MILDRED'S TEMPLE KITCHEN

OUT TO BRUNCH

PHOTOGRAPHS
DOUGLAS BRADSHAW AND EDWARD POND

PAINTINGS
HOLLY FARRELL

FOOD STYLING
CLAIRE STUBBS

TEXT
DONNA DOOHER AND CLAIRE STUBBS WITH LIANNE GEORGE

Published by: C.J. Oyster Publishing, Toronto
Written by: Donna Dooher & Claire Stubbs
Illustrated by: Holly Farrell
Photography by: Douglas Bradshaw, Edward Pond
Designed by: 52 Pick-up Inc., Toronto
Printed in Canada by: C.J. Graphics Inc. (Printers & Lithographers)

ISBN: 978-0-9783247-4-2

To
TED WHALEN
AND
IVAN LYNCH

FAIRY GODFATHERS

ON THE MENU

– CONTENTS –

A Word About Brunch

In 1990 we opened Mildred Pierce Restaurant in Toronto's industrial Queen Street West district. At Mildred Pierce, both the food and the atmosphere are elegant but comfortable, stylish but whimsical – like the title character of the novel by James M. Cain, as played by Joan Crawford in the 1945 film. This warm-hearted, hard-working gal with an old-fashioned culinary savvy and a spontaneous zest for life has given our restaurant its name and presides over it as patron spirit.

This cookbook recreates the experience of brunch at Mildred Pierce Restaurant and includes many of our favourite recipes, among them the signature dishes of each of the main characters in the film. In case you haven't seen it recently (or ever), here's the cast list:

Mildred Pierce Our heroine – a mother, a spurned wife and a wildly successful businesswoman who lives for her children and her restaurant.

Veda Pierce Mildred's ungrateful daughter, who longs for a life of wealth and privilege.

Bert Pierce Mildred's forlorn ex-husband – out of work, down on his luck and trying to quash rumours of his affair with Mrs. Biederhof.

Monty Beragon A self-proclaimed loaf and high-society sponge whose inheritance is running low. His dashing good looks and aristocratic airs catch the attention of both Mildred and her daughter Veda.

Wally Fay Bert Pierce's former business partner, in hot pursuit of Mildred and her restaurant empire.

Ida A sassy, headstrong, brazen dame who hires Mildred for her first job as a waitress. She becomes the loyal manager of Mildred's restaurant empire.

Maggie Biederhof The other woman.

Lottie Mildred's faithful maid, who has been with her from her humble beginnings.

We've divided the book into six chapters that follow the sequence of a Mildred Pierce brunch menu: Eye Openers (cocktails, hot beverages and fresh, fruity drinks to get you started); Teasers (warm, buttery baked goods to nibble on); A Dozen Eggs (twelve sensational egg dishes); Big Breakfast (hearty fare to take you through the day); "Let's Not Get Sticky About It" (sweet sweets); and Mildred's Pantry (a collection of must-have condiments). Special ingredients, unusual equipment and useful techniques are highlighted in the main text and explained in the Glossary.

Our selection of recipes opens the door to a wonderful food experience. You provide the rest: a love of luxurious food and the lazy days you need to enjoy it.

Welcome to the best of brunch at Mildred Pierce!

MILDRED
Got a drink handy?

IDA
You never used to drink during the day.

MILDRED
Never used to drink at all.
Just a little habit I picked up from men.

EYE OPENERS

Welcome to Mildred Pierce. Please, make yourself at home. May we start you off with something to drink? Something tall and chilled, or freshly squeezed, or hot and soothing? The wonderful thing about brunch is that the lines between breakfast, lunch and dinner have disappeared. Would you like a cocktail? At brunch it's never too early. How about something fruity? Or bubbly? Or sweet? Perhaps you'd like to begin your day with a jolt of coffee. How about the most decadent coffee you've ever tasted – with chocolate or liqueur topped with a dollop of fresh whipped cream? Go ahead. Indulge.

Mildred's Passion
Champagne Cocktail
SERVES 1 (BUT MORE FUN FOR 2)

Mildred Pierce was known to take the occasional drink to celebrate her triumphs or drown her miseries. This elegant, bubbly champagne cocktail is the perfect toasting companion. Enjoy with abandon.

½ fl oz	15 mL	passion fruit liqueur
¼ fl oz	8 mL	Triple Sec liqueur
4 fl oz	125 mL	chilled champagne
a few	a few	ripe blackberries

In a cocktail shaker filled with ice, shake together the passion fruit liqueur and Triple Sec. Strain into a chilled champagne flute, gingerly top with champagne and drop in some ripe blackberries.

Lottie's Loyalty
Champers and OJ
SERVES 1 FAITHFULLY

The ever-present champagne and orange juice at brunch is as reliable as Mildred's devoted, bubbly maid Lottie. When in season, try it with blood orange or tangerine juice.

3 fl oz	90 mL	fresh squeezed orange juice
3 fl oz	90 mL	chilled champagne or sparkling wine

Pour the orange juice into a chilled champagne flute. Carefully (and we mean carefully, because it has a tendency to overflow) top with the champagne or sparkling wine.

Toast your good fortune.

Veda's Revenge

Spritzy Raspberry Cocktail

SERVES 1 UNGRATEFUL DAUGHTER

Veda was Mildred's snobbish, high-maintenance daughter – a poseur who constantly berated her mother for her "common" sensibilities. This sophisticated cocktail would have suited Veda perfectly, if only because "framboise" sounds so utterly high class.

1½ fl oz	45 mL	vodka
¾ fl oz	25 mL	framboise liqueur
2 fl oz	60 mL	fresh squeezed ruby grapefruit juice
½ fl oz	15 mL	fresh squeezed lime juice
3 fl oz	90 mL	soda water
a few	a few	maraschino cherries with very long stems

Place the vodka, framboise, ruby grapefruit and lime juice in a cocktail shaker filled with ice. Shake vigorously and strain into a chilled cocktail glass. Top up with soda water and garnish with a cherry or two ... or three.

Bert's Back

Campari and Grapefruit Cooler

SERVES 1, BUT NOT FOR LONG

Even though Bert left Mildred for the saucy Mrs. Biederhof, he still came around every once in a while to check up on his ex and to pour himself a tall drink from her well-stocked liquor cabinet. We think this is a cocktail you'll come back to every now and then – whenever you crave a change from your usual.

1½ fl oz	45 mL	gin
½ fl oz	15 mL	Campari
2 fl oz	60 mL	fresh squeezed ruby grapefruit juice
5 fl oz	150 mL	sparkling Limonata

Fill a tall glass with ice. Add the gin, Campari and ruby grapefruit juice. Top up with Limonata.

Note: If there's any room left, garnish with more gin.

Bungalow Island Caesar

MAKES 1 RATHER HAPPY

In the summer, the gang at Mildred Pierce Restaurant heads off to a little island on Big Rideau Lake for a long weekend of unwinding and Caesars – lots of them. Rejuvenating and refreshing, it's the perfect late-morning hangover helper. This deluxe recipe, perfected by our staff after years and years of practice, is now a Mildred Pierce brunch classic.

1	1	lemon wedge
2 T	30 mL	kosher salt
6 fl oz	180 mL	Clamato
1½ fl oz	45 mL	vodka
10 drops	10 drops	Tabasco sauce
½ tsp	2 mL	Worcestershire sauce
¼ tsp	1 mL	celery seed, toasted
¼ tsp	1 mL	cracked black pepper
1 tsp	5 mL	horseradish, freshly grated
1	1	freshly shucked oyster (optional)
pinch	pinch	chives, finely chopped
1 stalk	1 stalk	celery

Run the lemon wedge around the rim of a tall glass, then dip the rim into the kosher salt.

Fill a cocktail shaker with ice and shake together the Clamato, vodka, Tabasco and Worcestershire. Strain into the glass.

Stir in the celery seed, pepper and horseradish. Drop in the freshly shucked oyster.

Garnish with chives and celery stalk.

Honeydew Lassi
Kind of a Smoothie
REFRESHES 6

Lassi is a chilled yogurt and coconut milk drink. Very popular in Asia, it's sold by vendors on bustling city streets as a cool refresher to subdue the effects of hot, spicy foods. Although we've chosen to use honeydew melon, lassi can be made with a variety of fruits – try mango, canteloupe, peaches or fresh berries.

¼ cup	60 mL	white sugar
¼ cup	60 mL	water
6 cups	1.5 L	honeydew melon (about 1), peeled and cubed
1¼ cups	310 mL	plain yogurt
½ cup	125 mL	coconut milk
2 tsp	10 mL	fresh squeezed lime juice

Combine the sugar and water in a stainless-steel saucepan. Boil for 2 minutes to make a syrup. Remove the saucepan from the heat and let the syrup cool completely.

In a blender or food processor, combine the syrup, honeydew melon, yogurt, coconut milk and lime juice. Blend until smooth and frothy.

Serve well chilled.

MILDRED SAYS

Why do you heat up sugar and water for a cold drink? This mixture is boiled briefly until it forms a syrup. These syrups are easy to incorporate into cold drinks and ensure that all the sugar crystals have completely dissolved and aren't sitting at the bottom of your glass.

Porch Swing Lemonade

MAKES 1 LARGE PITCHER

Here's a thought: Lemonade is the Norman Rockwell of fruit drinks. What other drink instantly conjures up sentimental images of balmy weather, porch swings and lazy afternoons? Ours is a simple recipe for real lemonade – guaranteed to take you back to your childhood lemonade stand. To make sparkling lemonade, substitute fizzy water for the regular cold water to finish.

1 cup	250 mL	white sugar
5 cups	1.25 L	cold water
1¼ cups	310 mL	fresh squeezed lemon juice (about 5 lemons)
a few	a few	mint sprigs

In a stainless-steel saucepan, combine the sugar and 1 cup (250 mL) of the water. Bring to a boil, stirring until the sugar has dissolved. Reduce the heat and simmer for 5 minutes. Remove the saucepan from the heat and let the sugar syrup cool completely.

Stir in the lemon juice and the remaining 4 cups (1 L) of water. Refrigerate the lemonade until cold.

Pour into tall glasses with plenty of ice and garnish with sprigs of mint.

Peachy Keen Iced Tea

MAKES 6 TALL GLASSES

If you've forgotten what authentic brewed iced tea is supposed to taste like, you're not the only one. This recipe is sweet, tart and utterly refreshing. On hot summer days we make pitcher after pitcher for our thirsty guests – it's so popular, we can hardly make it fast enough. And with the infinite variety of teas available – fruit, herbal and green – this summer favourite has endless possibilities.

¼ cup	60 mL	white sugar
5 cups	1.25 L	water
1 T	15 mL	orange pekoe tea, loose (or 2 bags)
1 tsp	5 mL	Earl Grey tea, loose (or 1 bag)
1 tsp	5 mL	mint tea, loose (or 1 bag)
1 cup	250 mL	peach juice
3 T	45 mL	fresh squeezed lemon juice
a few	a few	lemon slices

Combine the sugar and water in a stainless-steel saucepan and bring to a boil. Remove from the heat.

Add the teas and peach and lemon juices to the saucepan and leave to steep for 30 minutes. Strain the tea and refrigerate until cold.

Serve in tall glasses with plenty of ice and lemon slices.

Mildred Says

You don't have to keep your citrus fruits in the refrigerator – after all, they come from the tropics. You'll get more juice from your lemons, limes and oranges if they're not cold. Loosen them up by rolling them around on the countertop before squeezing.

White Hot Mocha

FILLS 4 "CAFÉ AU LAIT" BOWLS

We think of our White Hot Mocha as a modern-day temptress with old-fashioned values. The sublime marriage of espresso and brandy tempers the sweetness of the white chocolate and gives this warm drink a touch of seduction.

1	1	vanilla bean
3 cups	750 mL	2% milk
1 cup	250 mL	35% cream
4 oz	115 g	best-quality white chocolate, finely chopped
½ cup	125 mL	brewed espresso coffee
2 fl oz	60 mL	brandy

Split the vanilla bean lengthwise and scrape out the seeds.

Combine the vanilla bean, vanilla seeds, milk and cream in a stainless-steel saucepan and bring to a boil. Remove the saucepan from the heat, take out the vanilla bean and whisk in the white chocolate, espresso and brandy.

Pour the White Hot Mocha into warm café au lait bowls and dip with Double-Crossed Biscotti (see page 96).

Wally's Dealmaker

Boozy Coffee

MAKES 1 BIG DEAL

Wally was only too happy to offer Mildred advice on matters of business and romance, sometimes bringing along a bottle of bourbon for inspiration. This warm, sweet, bourbon-infused coffee is a great mood setter for sharing intimate secrets.

1 T	15 mL	white sugar
½ tsp	2 mL	ground cinnamon
1	1	orange wedge
1½ fl oz	45 mL	bourbon
6 fl oz	180 mL	fresh brewed coffee
¼ cup	60 mL	whipped cream
½ fl oz	15 mL	crème de cacao liqueur

Combine the sugar and cinnamon in a shallow dish. Run the orange wedge around the rim of a heat-proof glass and dip the rim into the cinnamon sugar.

Pour in the bourbon and coffee, float whipped cream on top and drizzle with crème de cacao.

MILDRED SAYS
Coffee, chocolate, men ... some things are just better rich.

MILDRED
You can talk your way out of anything, can't you Wally?
You're good at that.

WALLY
In my business you have to be.
Only right now, I'd rather talk myself into something – know what I mean?

TEASERS

Now that you've settled in and ordered a drink, you must be getting ravenous. How about something to nibble on while we prepare your main dish? We've got quite a selection of warm, buttery treats hot from our oven – homemade breads, scones and biscuits just waiting to be slathered with one of our flavoured butters or homemade preserves, not to mention our heavenly granola made with coconut and macadamia nuts. Sweet or savoury, we have something to whet your appetite. But don't just take our word for it. You be the judge.

Mildred's Scones

MAKES A DOZEN

A scone is warm, glorious comfort food made with simple, wholesome ingredients best enjoyed on a slow Sunday morning over coffee and a thick newspaper. At Mildred Pierce Restaurant we're renowned for our flaky, buttery scones served with Strawberry Fruit Butter (see Mildred's Pantry, page 105). Our brunch guests have been requesting the recipe for years. And, for the record, there's no such thing as a low-fat scone.

3 cups	750 mL	all-purpose flour
2 tsp	10 mL	baking powder
½ tsp	2 mL	baking soda
⅓ cup	75 mL	white sugar
¼ tsp	1 mL	salt
½ cup	125 mL	unsalted butter, cold
½ cup	125 mL	shortening, cold
⅓ cup	75 mL	dried black currants
1 T	15 mL	grated lemon zest
1 cup	235 mL	35% cream

Preheat the oven to 400°F (200°C).

In a large bowl, sift together the flour, baking powder, baking soda, sugar and salt.

Using a coarse cheese grater, grate the unsalted butter into the dry ingredients. Add the shortening, and with your fingertips break it up into small pieces. Combine the mixture with your hands until it resembles cornmeal. Stir in the currants and lemon zest. Add the cream, gently working the mixture until the flour is incorporated and the dough forms a ball.

Turn the dough out onto a lightly floured surface and gently roll out to a 1" (2.5 cm) thickness. Dip a 2" (5 cm) round cookie cutter into some flour and stamp out the scones. Press any scraps together and again pat into a 1" (2.5 cm) thickness. Cut out the remaining scones.

To bake, place the scones 2" (5 cm) apart on a parchment paper–lined baking sheet. Lightly brush the tops with some 35% cream and sprinkle with a little sugar.

Bake for 15 to 18 minutes on the top rack of the oven until the scones are lightly golden on the outside, fluffy on the inside. Best served hot from the oven.

Mildred Says

The highly flavoured natural oil of citrus fruit is in the coloured peel, or zest. The zest is added to impart an intense flavour to baked goods, vinaigrettes and sauces. There are many ways to remove the zest from citrus fruit, but the tricky part is to avoid the bitter white pith that lies beneath the outer peel. The most effective method we've found is to use a fine grater or rasp. Our rasp of choice is a carpenter's micro-plane wood rasp – a file with many sharp, tiny teeth (also handy for mincing ginger, garlic and horseradish).

Best Buttermilk Biscuits

MAKES A DOZEN

A generation ago, just about everyone (okay, every woman) knew how to make fresh biscuits. It was taken for granted that lunch or dinner would be accompanied by rolls or biscuits hot from the oven. But since the advent of TV dinners and microwaveable entrées, we seem to have forgotten that there's nothing complicated about making these simple luxuries. Try these biscuits with Red Pepper Jelly or our delicious Peach and Amaretto Jam (see Mildred's Pantry, page 104).

1 T	15 mL	fresh yeast
1 T	15 mL	warm water
3 cups	750 mL	all-purpose flour
2 tsp	10 mL	baking powder
½ tsp	2 mL	baking soda
2 tsp	10 mL	white sugar
1 tsp	5 mL	salt
1 cup	235 mL	unsalted butter, cold
1 cup	235 mL	buttermilk
2 T	30 mL	unsalted butter, melted

Preheat the oven to 400°F (200°C).

Wake up your yeast by dissolving it in the warm water. Once it's foamy, in about 5 minutes, it's ready to use.

Sift the flour, baking powder, baking soda, sugar and salt into a separate bowl. Using a coarse cheese grater, grate the cold butter into the dry ingredients and combine with your fingertips until the texture is crumbly.

Add the buttermilk and the yeast mixture, and mix all the ingredients together until the dough forms a ball.

Turn the dough out onto a lightly floured surface and knead gently until smooth, about 2 minutes. Roll the dough out to a 1" (2.5 cm) thickness. Dust a sharp knife with some flour and cut the biscuits into 2" (5 cm) squares.

To bake, place the biscuits 2" (5 cm) apart on a parchment paper–lined baking sheet. Brush the tops with melted butter. Bake on the top rack of the oven for 15 to 18 minutes until puffed and lightly golden.

MILDRED SAYS

Just little ol' you for brunch, and you can't eat all 12 biscuits? Place the unbaked biscuits or scones on a parchment paper–lined baking sheet and pop into the freezer. When they're frozen through, transfer them to a freezer bag or tightly sealed container. As the craving strikes, take some out of the freezer, place on a tray and defrost completely in the refrigerator before baking.

Cheddar Thyme Biscuits

MAKES A DOZEN

Thyme works beautifully to flavour savoury baked goods. This hearty herb stands up to the preparation of these biscuits without losing its woodsy, aromatic flavour. Fresh from the oven, you just can't beat these cheesy, herbed biscuits with a slathering of our Tomato Butter (see Mildred's Pantry, page 105).

2 cups	500 mL	all-purpose flour
1 T	15 mL	baking powder
1 tsp	5 mL	salt
¾ cup	175 mL	unsalted butter, cold
¼ cup	60 mL	fresh thyme, finely chopped
¾ cup	175 mL	aged cheddar cheese, grated
2 large	2 large	eggs
½ cup	120 mL	35% cream

Preheat the oven to 375°F (190°C).

In a large bowl, combine the flour, baking powder and salt. Using a coarse cheese grater, grate the cold butter into the dry ingredients. With your hands, combine the mixture until it resembles cornmeal. Stir in the fresh thyme and cheddar cheese.

In a small bowl, whisk together the eggs and cream. Pour the wet ingredients into the dry ingredients and combine until the dough forms a ball.

Turn the dough out onto a lightly floured surface and roll out to a 1" (2.5 cm) thickness. Dust a sharp knife with some flour and cut the biscuits into 2" (5 cm) squares.

Arrange the biscuits 2" (5 cm) apart on a parchment paper–lined baking sheet. Bake on the top rack of the oven for 20 to 25 minutes until lightly golden.

MILDRED SAYS

To prolong the life of your fresh herbs, wrap each bunch snugly in damp paper towels and store in plastic bags in the refrigerator. Hearty herbs like rosemary and thyme and delicate, leafy herbs like tarragon and basil will stay fresher much longer.

Bacon and Asiago Crumpets

MAKES A DOZEN

You don't often hear of people making crumpets from scratch, but ours are so much better than any you'll ever buy. Tear open these toasty, bubbly crumpets with a fork to ensure that butter gets into each little nook and cranny. Or serve them with poached eggs on top and let them soak up all the yolk.

Before You Start …
For this recipe you'll need crumpet rings or round metal cookie cutters, 3 1/2" (9 cm) in diameter and 2" (5 cm) deep.

1½ cups	355 mL	2% milk
1½ tsp	7 mL	white sugar
2 T	30 mL	fresh yeast
2½ cups	625 mL	all-purpose flour
pinch	pinch	salt
½ tsp	2 mL	baking soda
6½ fl oz	195 mL	water
¾ cup	175 mL	Asiago cheese, grated
¼ cup	60 mL	crispy cooked bacon (4 slices), chopped
¼ cup	60 mL	shallots, minced
1½ tsp	7 mL	kosher salt
1 T	15 mL	Italian parsley, finely chopped
⅓ cup	75 mL	unsalted butter, melted

In a small saucepan, heat the milk until just warm. Stir in the sugar and yeast and let stand for 10 minutes.

In a bowl, combine the flour and the pinch of salt and mix in the yeast mixture. Cover and let stand in a warm place (like the top of your refrigerator) for an hour or until doubled in size.

Mix the baking soda with the water and pour into the batter. Beat vigorously with a wooden spoon. Fold in the cheese, crispy bacon, shallots, kosher salt and parsley.

Brush a large nonstick skillet and 4 crumpet rings or metal cookie cutters with the melted butter. Place the rings in the skillet over medium-high heat. Fill each ring with 1/3 cup (75 mL) of batter. Reduce the heat to low and cook for 5 minutes until the surface of the batter is full of large bubbles. Carefully remove the hot rings and gently turn the crumpets over. Cook for 5 more minutes.

If you're making crumpets faster than you're eating them, keep them warm in a 250°F (120°C) oven.

Irish Soda Bread

MAKES 1 LOAF

Soda bread is a quick and easy one-step bread. Just mix all the ingredients together, shape the loaf and put it in the oven. We've preserved the Irish tradition of slashing a big X on the top of the loaf, not only to ensure even baking but also to keep the devil at bay (always desirable when perfecting the finicky art of baking). Try a slice with a dollop of Red Pepper Jelly (see Mildred's Pantry, page 104) and a thick wedge of cheddar cheese.

2 cups	500 mL	whole-wheat flour
1½ cups	375 mL	all-purpose flour
½ cup	125 mL	old-fashioned rolled oats
2 T	30 mL	brown sugar, packed
2 tsp	10 mL	salt
1 tsp	5 mL	baking soda
1 tsp	5 mL	baking powder
3 T	45 mL	unsalted butter, cold
1½ cups	355 mL	buttermilk
1 large	1 large	egg

Preheat the oven to 350°F (180°C).

In a large bowl, combine the whole-wheat flour, all-purpose flour, rolled oats, brown sugar, salt, baking soda and baking powder. Using a cheese grater, grate the cold butter into the dry ingredients and blend by hand until the mixture resembles cornmeal.

In a small bowl, whisk together the buttermilk and egg, then pour into the dry ingredients. Using your hands, combine the dry and wet ingredients together until the dough forms a ball.

Turn the dough out onto a lightly floured surface and knead for 5 minutes until soft and elastic. Shape into a round loaf 6" (15 cm) in diameter and place on a parchment paper–lined baking sheet.

Dust the top of the loaf with a little flour and, with a sharp knife, cut a large X into the top, 1/2 the depth of the loaf and to within 1" (2.5 cm) of the edge.

Bake for 45 to 50 minutes, at which point the loaf should sound hollow when you tap the bottom.

Mildred Says

Rubberized silicone mats are an alternative to parchment paper for lining baking sheets. These handy nonstick mats are reusable, withstand high heat and are perfect for baking cookies, scones, biscuits and profiteroles. They come in a variety of sizes and are readily available at most kitchen supply stores.

Perfect Breakfast Brioche

MAKES 2 LOAVES

Brioche is a rich, yeasted bread made with butter and eggs – one of the most decadent and versatile breads around. It takes some time to prepare, but the result is well worth the effort. At Mildred Pierce Restaurant we use brioche to make Ida's Famous French Toast and our Roasted Pepper and Basil Strata, but it's also great sliced up, warm from the oven, with our Chocolate Pecan Smother (see Mildred's Pantry, page 106).

2 T	30 mL	fresh yeast
5 T	75 mL	water, room temperature
6 large	6 large	eggs
3½ cups	875 mL	all-purpose flour
4½ T	67 mL	white sugar
1 tsp	5 mL	salt
1½ cups	375 mL	unsalted butter, soft
2 T	30 mL	unsalted butter, melted

In the bowl of an electric stand mixer fitted with a dough hook, mix the yeast, water and eggs on low speed until well combined.

In a separate bowl, combine the flour, sugar and salt, then add to the yeast mixture. Mix on low speed for 5 minutes until fully incorporated. The dough will be smooth and sticky. Scrape down the sides of the bowl with a spatula and continue mixing for 5 more minutes. Increase the speed to medium and drop in small pieces of the soft butter, combining well after each addition. Continue to mix until all the butter disappears into the dough.

Scrape the dough out into a large bowl. Cover with plastic wrap and set in a warm place (like the top of your refrigerator) to rise for 2 hours or until the dough has doubled in size.

Punch down and deflate the dough in the bowl. Rewrap and refrigerate the dough for 3 hours.

Preheat the oven to 375°F (190°C).

Butter 2 loaf pans 8 1/2" x 4 1/2" x 2 3/4" (22 cm x 11.5 cm x 7 cm).

Divide the dough into 2 equal pieces and place in the prepared loaf pans or brioche moulds. Cover each pan with plastic wrap and set in a warm place to rise. The dough is ready to bake when it has tripled in size and completely fills the pan, after about 2 hours.

Brush the top of each loaf with the melted butter. Bake for 25 to 30 minutes.

Remove the loaves from the oven and cool for 5 minutes. Turn the loaves out and cool completely.

MILDRED SAYS

Hands are your best tools in the kitchen. Don't be afraid to take off your diamonds, roll up your sleeves and get right in there. When punching down sticky soft doughs, try dusting your hands lightly with flour first to keep more dough in the bowl and less on your hands.

Banana, Date and Pecan Muffins

MAKES A DOZEN

The best muffins are bursting with flavour and made with natural, wholesome ingredients. Break open these quick, comforting treats straight from the oven and slather them with our homemade Apple Cardamom Butter (see Mildred's Pantry, page 106).

2 cups	500 mL	all-purpose flour
1 cup	250 mL	white sugar
½ tsp	2 mL	baking soda
¾ tsp	4 mL	baking powder
½ tsp	2 mL	salt
1 tsp	5 mL	ground cinnamon
¾ cup	175 mL	old-fashioned rolled oats
2 large	2 large	eggs
¾ cup	175 mL	plain yogurt
½ cup	125 mL	vegetable oil
2 T	30 mL	unsalted butter, melted
½ tsp	2 mL	vanilla extract
1¼ cups	310 mL	ripe bananas, mashed (about 3 bananas)
¾ cup	175 mL	pecan halves, chopped
¾ cup	175 mL	dates, chopped

Preheat the oven to 350°F (180°C).

In a large bowl, combine the flour, sugar, baking soda, baking powder, salt, cinnamon and rolled oats.

In a separate bowl, combine the eggs, yogurt, vegetable oil, melted butter, vanilla extract and bananas.

Beat the wet ingredients into the dry ingredients with a wooden spoon, then fold in the pecans and dates.

Spoon the batter into standard muffin tins (either buttered or lined with paper muffin cups). Fill each cup to the top. Bake for 18 to 20 minutes, until muffins are puffed and golden.

MILDRED SAYS

We're most familiar with bottled vanilla extract, but today we can buy whole **vanilla beans** (though these little treasures are costly) and capture a true vanilla flavour. Choose soft, plump beans and store in an airtight container. Most recipes call for the bean to be split lengthwise and the tiny black seeds exposed to maximize flavour. Seeds are added directly to sauces, cakes and custards while whole beans or pods are used to infuse liquids. These pods can be used again when rinsed and dried. Make an intense vanilla sugar by burying the pods in a jar of white sugar and leaving to infuse for a week or two. Use the vanilla sugar to sweeten baked goods or your morning coffee.

Cinnamon Sugar Beignets
Doughnuts by Any Other Name
MAKES A DOZEN

Beignets don't have a hole in the middle, but you'll recognize the taste. Rolled in Cinnamon Sugar, these treats should be eaten while they're still warm. They're great on their own or dunked into coffee. Magnifique!

CINNAMON SUGAR

1 cup	250 mL	white sugar
1 tsp	5 mL	ground cinnamon

In a small, shallow bowl, stir together the sugar and cinnamon and set aside for doughnut rolling.

BEIGNET DOUGH

½ cup	125 mL	warm water
2 T	30 mL	fresh yeast
2 T	30 mL	white sugar
¼ cup	60 mL	unsalted butter, soft
2 tsp	10 mL	ground cinnamon
2 large	2 large	eggs
1 large	1 large	egg yolk
½ tsp	2 mL	salt
1⅔ cups	400 mL	all-purpose flour
		vegetable oil for deep-frying

In a bowl, combine the warm water, yeast and 1 tsp (5 mL) of the sugar. Set in a warm place for 10 minutes.

In a large bowl, cream together the butter, remaining white sugar and the cinnamon. Add the eggs and yolk one at a time, beating well with a wooden spoon after each addition. Beat in the yeast mixture, salt and flour until smooth.

Cover the bowl with plastic wrap and place in a warm spot until the dough has doubled in size, about 2 hours. Punch down the dough in the bowl, cover again and refrigerate for 3 hours or overnight.

We recommend a deep-fryer to fry the beignets, but you could also use a deep pot filled to no more than 4" (10 cm) from the top with vegetable oil.

Heat the oil to 325°F (160°C). Meanwhile, turn the dough out onto a lightly floured surface and press to a 1" (2.5 cm) thickness. Using a 2" (5 cm) cookie cutter dipped into flour, stamp out the beignets. Press scraps together and pat into a 1" (2.5 cm) thickness. Cut out the remaining beignets.

Fry beignets, 4 at a time, turning occasionally until they're evenly browned (about 5 minutes). With the slotted spoon or spider, carefully scoop them out and place on a paper towel to absorb any excess oil. Roll the beignets in the Cinnamon Sugar while they're still warm.

Crunchy Coconut Macadamia Granola with Honey

MAKES 5 CUPS (1.25 L)

Granola might not be enough to entice you out of bed in the morning, but our decadent Coconut Macadamia Granola will beckon you from the cupboard and wake you from your lazy slumber. So get out of bed and treat yourself to a big bowl heaped with plenty of fresh fruit and yogurt.

½ cup	125 mL	unsalted sunflower seeds
½ cup	125 mL	pumpkin seeds
½ cup	125 mL	slivered almonds
½ cup	125 mL	unsweetened shredded coconut
¼ cup	60 mL	oat bran
2 cups	500 mL	old-fashioned rolled oats
½ tsp	2 mL	ground cinnamon
½ tsp	2 mL	ground ginger
½ cup	125 mL	unsalted butter
½ cup	125 mL	honey
1 tsp	5 mL	orange oil
1 cup	250 mL	macadamia nuts
½ cup	125 mL	dried black currants
½ cup	125 mL	dried apricots, sliced

Preheat the oven to 350°F (180°C).

Spread the sunflower seeds, pumpkin seeds and almonds on a baking sheet and toast in the oven for 5 minutes. Add the coconut to the baking sheet and toast for 5 more minutes. Remove from the oven and set aside to cool.

Reduce the oven temperature to 300°F (150°C).

In a large bowl, combine the oat bran, rolled oats, cinnamon and ginger.

In a small saucepan, melt the butter over low heat and stir in the honey and orange oil. Pour over the oat mixture, stirring well to combine.

Spread the oat mixture on a parchment paper–lined baking sheet. Place the baking sheet in the oven, and after 20 minutes stir the mixture with a wooden spoon (this ensures that it will brown evenly). Continue baking for 10 more minutes.

Remove from the oven and let the oat mixture cool completely on the baking sheet. The mixture will harden as it cools. With your hands, break the oat mixture up into small pieces. Add the macadamia nuts, coconut mixture, currants and apricots.

To keep its crunch, store the granola in an airtight container.

MILDRED
And just what do you do, Mr. Beragon?
MONTY
I loaf – though in a decorative and highly charming manner.

A DOZEN EGGS

Brunch is all about pandering to your eating whims. It may be one, two or even three o'clock in the afternoon, but if you're craving bacon and eggs, go for it. Or how about one of our deluxe egg dishes? Eggs are the beloved breakfast staple, and here we've paired them with an array of fresh ingredients – herbs, sauces and creamy, decadent cheeses. Our Mollycoddled Eggs are warm and comforting, the Huevos Monty will satisfy the biggest appetite and the kids will love Green Eggs and Ham. Brunch is definitely more than just a late breakfast.

Veda's Choice

SERVES 2

This dolled-up version of eggs Benedict is sinfully extravagant – perfect for the vampy Veda. Picture two gently poached eggs perched delicately on slices of the finest Atlantic smoked salmon, smothered in velvety Béarnaise Sauce and served on a buttery croissant. So rich, it's scandalous. You'll love it almost as much as Veda would!

BÉARNAISE SAUCE

½ cup	125 mL	white wine
½ cup	125 mL	unsalted butter
4 large	4 large	egg yolks
2 T	30 mL	shallots, minced
2 T	30 mL	fresh tarragon, chopped
¾ tsp	4 mL	kosher salt
2 tsp	10 mL	fresh squeezed lemon juice

Place the white wine in a small stainless-steel saucepan. Bring to a boil, then lower the heat to medium and simmer for 5 minutes until the wine has reduced by half.

Meanwhile, bring the butter to a boil and carefully skim any foam from the surface.

Place the egg yolks in a stainless-steel bowl and whisk in the wine reduction. Slowly drizzle in the hot butter, whisking constantly until fully incorporated.

Bring a pot of water to the boil and then remove it from the heat. Place the bowl, with the eggs and butter mixture, over the pot. (Make sure the bottom of the bowl isn't touching the water or the eggs may curdle.) Whisk constantly until the sauce is smooth and has thickened just enough to coat the back of a spoon, about 1 1/2 minutes. Cooking for too long may result in a less than velvety sauce that's too thick to coat the eggs.

Stir in the shallots, tarragon, salt and lemon juice.

PUTTING IT ALL TOGETHER

2	2	croissants
2 slices	2 slices	Atlantic smoked salmon
4 large	4 large	eggs, poached

Preheat the oven to 300°F (150°C).

Using a serrated knife, slice the croissants in half horizontally and place the tops and bottoms on a baking sheet and into the oven to warm.

To serve, lay a slice of smoked salmon on the bottom half of a warm croissant and nestle 2 poached eggs on top. Generously spoon the warm Béarnaise Sauce over the eggs and replace the croissant top.

Mildred Says

To poach eggs, bring a large pot of salted water to a boil. Add a splash of white vinegar and reduce the heat to a gentle simmer. (The vinegar helps to keep the egg whites together.) Crack an egg into a small cup, taking care not to break the yolk. Slip the egg into the simmering water. An egg poached for 2 to 3 minutes will have a delicate, runny yolk and a tender white. Use a slotted spoon to retrieve the eggs, which will help drain away the excess water. For poaching more than 1 egg, allow plenty of room for them to move around and try to remove them from the pot in the order that they went in to ensure consistent cooking times.

Mollycoddled Eggs

SERVES 4

Coddled and indulged – these two words define Veda's relationship with Mildred. Our pampered eggs are baked with spinach and mushrooms on a soft bed of creamy Lemon Polenta smothered in velvety Gorgonzola Sauce. Treat yourself.

BEFORE YOU START...
For this recipe you'll need 4 ramekins, with 1 cup (250 mL) capacity.

LEMON POLENTA

½ cup	125 mL	water
½ cup	125 mL	2% milk
½ cup	125 mL	35% cream
½ tsp	2 mL	kosher salt
¼ cup	60 mL	quick-cook cornmeal
2 tsp	10 mL	grated lemon zest

In a large pot, combine the water, milk, cream and salt and bring to a boil. Reduce the heat to low and in a slow, steady stream pour in the cornmeal, stirring constantly with a wooden spoon. Cook for at least 5 minutes, still stirring, until thickened. Mix in the lemon zest. Divide the lemon polenta evenly among the 4 ramekins.

SPINACH AND MUSHROOMS

2 T	30 mL	unsalted butter
2 cups	500 mL	white mushrooms, thinly sliced
¼ cup	60 mL	shallots, finely chopped
1 tsp	5 mL	fresh thyme, finely chopped
½ tsp	2 mL	kosher salt
1 cup	250 mL	spinach leaves, chiffonade

Over medium-high heat, melt the butter and sauté the mushrooms and shallots until tender. Add the thyme and salt. Divide the spinach between each polenta-filled ramekin and top with the mushroom mixture.

GORGONZOLA SAUCE

1 cup	250 mL	35% cream
¼ cup	60 mL	Gorgonzola cheese
1 T	15 mL	all-purpose flour
pinch	pinch	ground nutmeg
pinch	pinch	cayenne pepper

In a small saucepan, bring the cream to a boil. Reduce the heat to low and add the Gorgonzola, stirring until melted and smooth. Whisk in the flour, nutmeg and cayenne and cook for 2 more minutes. Set aside.

PUTTING IT ALL TOGETHER

4 large	4 large	eggs
½ tsp	2 mL	kosher salt

Preheat the oven to 325°F (160°C). Make a shallow indent in the mushroom mixture using the back of a tablespoon. Crack 1 egg into each indent and smother with Gorgonzola Sauce. Place the ramekins on a baking sheet and bake for 25 minutes. Baked eggs should have whites that are just set, but yolks that are still runny.

MILDRED SAYS
A chiffonade is a classic cut that's great for delicate leafy herbs and greens like basil and spinach. It keeps the leaves brilliant green and aromatic. To chiffonade, stack the leaves 5 or 6 high and, with a very sharp knife, slice into fine ribbons.

Omelette with Chanterelles and St. André

MAKES 1

Chances are you've had a simple mushroom and cheese omelette, but until you've tried this hoity-toity version you won't know how truly fabulous an omelette can be. Here we've paired chanterelles (a trumpet-shaped wild mushroom with an earthy, nutty taste) with St. André (a decadent French triple-cream cheese). Make sure to serve piping hot straight from the pan. A fine omelette waits for no one.

CHANTERELLE FILLING

1 T	15 mL	unsalted butter
1 T	15 mL	shallots, minced
¼ cup	60 mL	chanterelle mushrooms, cleaned and sliced
pinch	pinch	kosher salt
pinch	pinch	cracked black pepper
2 T	30 mL	St. André cheese, cut into small pieces

In a small skillet, melt the butter over medium-high heat until it starts to bubble. Add the shallots, cooking until soft, and then add the chanterelles and cook for 2 more minutes. Season with salt and pepper and keep warm while you prepare the omelette.

PUTTING IT ALL TOGETHER

3 large	3 large	eggs
2 T	30 mL	35% cream
pinch	pinch	kosher salt
pinch	pinch	cracked black pepper
1 tsp	5 mL	unsalted butter

In a small bowl, whisk together the eggs, cream, salt and pepper.

Set an 8" (20 cm) omelette pan over high heat. Once the pan is good and hot, add the butter.

When the butter starts to sizzle, add in the egg mixture all at once. With a high-heat spatula, stir slowly for 15 to 20 seconds, as though you were making scrambled eggs. Reduce the heat to medium, and sprinkle the warm chanterelles and the St. André over half of the omelette. As soon as the egg is just set on the bottom, after about 1 minute, fold the omelette in half to enclose the filling.

Tilt the pan to slide the omelette out onto a warm plate. The omelette should be fluffy and light golden on the outside and soft and moist on the inside. Serve without delay.

Mildred Says

The secret to cooking a great omelette is in the pan. An omelette pan has a flat, heavy bottom for even cooking and low, sloping sides to allow the omelette to roll out. Stainless-steel and cast-iron omelette pans need to be **seasoned** for optimum use (some pans come with nonstick finishes). Serious cooks usually reserve their omelette pans for egg cooking only and never wash off the desired patina with soap and water. The pans are just wiped clean and brushed with a light coat of vegetable oil.

Green Eggs and Ham

Spinach Scrambled Eggs

SERVES 4 "SAM I AMS"

"Would you like them here and there? Would you like them anywhere?" Inspired by Dr. Seuss's classic *Green Eggs and Ham*, this is one of the most popular items on our brunch menu. It not only tastes great, but, well, it's just fun. Fresh spinach turns the scrambled eggs a vibrant green. A thick slice of grilled country ham, Rosemary Roasted Potatoes and warm Cheddar Thyme Biscuits (see pages 27, 64) complete the story.

2½ cups	625 mL	spinach leaves, tightly packed
12 large	12 large	eggs
1 tsp	5 mL	kosher salt
2 T	30 mL	unsalted butter
4 thick slices		country-style ham

Blanch the spinach. Drain and squeeze out all excess water from the spinach as if you were squeezing a sponge.

In a blender or food processor, purée the spinach with the eggs and salt until smooth.

Drop 1 T (15 mL) of the butter into a hot skillet and fry the slices of ham until they're golden. Keep warm while preparing the green eggs.

Melt the remaining butter in a large omelette pan over medium heat. When the butter starts to sizzle, add the green eggs all at once. Stir gently with a high-heat spatula, keeping the eggs in constant motion until they begin to set. As soon as they're cooked, remove the pan from the heat (ideally, scrambled eggs should be soft, moist and fluffy).

Arrange slices of grilled ham on warm plates and pile on the green eggs.

MILDRED SAYS

When cracking eggs, gently rap the egg on a flat surface or countertop, not on the side of a bowl, to get a good even break. Break the eggs into a bowl instead of directly into the pan – that way, if there are little pieces of shell, you can retrieve them easily.

Huevos Monty

SERVES 6

Named for Monty Beragon, the spicy Latin playboy who swept Mildred Pierce off her feet. Our take on huevos rancheros is a hearty concoction of Black Bean Refritos and sharp cheddar layered between flour tortillas, topped with eggs sunny-side up and garnished with fresh Tomato Salsa and Avocado Crema. This dish is almost impossible to resist – just like Monty.

BLACK BEAN REFRITOS

2 cups	500 mL	dried black beans
½ cup	125 mL	olive oil
3 cups	750 mL	onion, finely chopped
1 T	15 mL	garlic, minced
4 tsp	20 mL	ground coriander
4 tsp	20 mL	ground cumin
½ tsp	2 mL	chili powder
1 T	15 mL	kosher salt

Soak the black beans overnight in plenty of water. The next morning, drain and cook with 8 cups (2 mL) of cold water until they are very soft, about 40 minutes. Drain, reserving 1/2 cup (125 mL) of the liquid.

In a large pot, heat the olive oil over medium-high heat. Sauté the onion and garlic until soft and fragrant. Stir in the coriander, cumin, chili powder and salt, and cook for 5 more minutes. Add the black beans and the reserved liquid. Cook for 2 more minutes while stirring constantly. In a food processor, purée 1/2 the bean mixture until smooth. Transfer the purée to a mixing bowl and stir in the remaining whole beans.

PUTTING IT ALL TOGETHER

12	12	soft flour tortillas, about 8" (20 cm) round
3 cups	750 mL	aged cheddar, grated
1 recipe	1 recipe	Tomato Salsa (see Mildred's Pantry, page 112)
12 large	12 large	eggs, fried sunny-side up
¾ cup	175 mL	sour cream
1 recipe	1 recipe	Avocado Crema (see Mildred's Pantry, page 113)

Preheat the oven to 350°F (180°C).

Lay out 6 tortillas on a baking sheet. Spread each tortilla with about 2/3 of a cup (150 mL) of Black Bean Refritos. On top of the refritos, sprinkle 1/2 cup (125 mL) of cheese and 2 T (30 mL) of Tomato Salsa. Bake the tortillas in the oven until the beans and salsa are warmed through and the cheese has melted. Top with the remaining 6 tortillas. Turn off the oven, but leave the tortillas in to keep warm while you prepare the eggs.

Over high heat, melt the butter in an omelette pan. Crack 2 eggs into a small bowl, being careful not to break the yolks. Slip the eggs into the pan, season with salt and pepper and reduce the heat to low. Ideally, sunny-side eggs should have a white that is crispy around the edges and a runny yolk that is just beginning to set.

Remove the tortillas from the oven and place each one on a warm plate. Slide sunny-side eggs on top of each one and garnish with spoonfuls of Tomato Salsa, sour cream and Avocado Crema.

Mildred Says

Menu planning and advance preparation can make cooking for the gang a stress-free experience. Huevos Monty, for example, is made up of several simple steps, some of which can be done in advance – the cheese grated and the Black Bean Refritos cooked. That way the Monty is easily assembled when your guests arrive.

Hole in One
Really Easy Over Egg in Toast
SERVES 4

Nearly everyone remembers this dish from childhood. There are almost as many names for it as there are versions – egg in the hole, eggs in a nest, spit in the ocean. Whatever you call it, you'll want to try our version made with crusty, cheddar cheese sourdough bread. Serve with slices of bacon and lots of Spicy Chipotle Ketchup (see Mildred's Pantry, page 111).

3 T	45 mL	unsalted butter, soft
4 slices	4 slices	cheddar cheese sourdough bread, 1" (2.5 cm) thick
4 large	4 large	eggs
½ tsp	2 mL	kosher salt
pinch	pinch	cracked black pepper

Butter both sides of the bread slices. Using a 2" (5 cm) round cookie cutter, cut a hole in the centre of each slice, reserving the "hole."

Melt some butter in a large skillet over medium heat. Lay the holes in the skillet and cook each side until golden brown. Remove and keep warm. Lay the bread slices in the skillet and crack an egg into the centre of each slice, being careful to keep the yolk intact. Season the eggs with salt and pepper.

Fry for 2 minutes, until the bread begins to toast on the bottom. Flip them over gently and fry for a further 2 minutes, until the whites are beginning to crisp but the yolk is still soft.

To eat, dip the fried holes into the runny yolks.

Mildred Says
We don't mean to complicate this uncomplicated recipe, but some common-sense pointers never hurt. The loaf needs to be sliced into large enough pieces to accommodate the 2" (5 cm) hole for the egg. If you're using a thin baguette, cut on a sharp diagonal to enlarge the surface area of the slice. Also make sure that the pan you're cooking in has a flat bottom to prevent the egg from running out of the hole.

Chorizo Tortilla with Picante Sauce

SERVES 4 TO 6

This traditional Spanish dish is a little bit omelette, a little bit frittata. Layers of potato, onions and chorizo (a spicy, smoked pork sausage) are combined with eggs and baked in a cast-iron skillet. Dish it up in big wedges with our Picante Sauce (see Mildred's Pantry, page 114) and a simple green salad.

2½ cups	625 mL	Yukon Gold potatoes, about 3, peeled and sliced ¼" (6 mm) thick
1 T	15 mL	olive oil
1 cup	250 mL	red onion, thinly sliced
1 cup	250 mL	chorizo, chopped
8 large	8 large	eggs
1 tsp	5 mL	kosher salt
½ tsp	2 mL	cracked black pepper
1 tsp	5 mL	fresh thyme, finely chopped
2 T	30 mL	vegetable oil

Preheat the oven to 350°F (180°C).

Place the sliced potatoes in a large pot. Fill with cold, well-salted water and bring to a boil, cooking for 1 minute. Remove the pot from the heat and let the potatoes stand for 5 minutes before draining. (This gentle cooking method helps keep the potato slices intact.)

Meanwhile, heat a seasoned 10" (25 cm) cast-iron skillet with an ovenproof handle over medium-high heat. Add the olive oil and sauté the onions and chorizo until the onions are soft, about 5 minutes. With a slotted spoon, transfer the onions and chorizo to a bowl and let cool slightly. Clean the skillet for the tortilla.

Crack the eggs into a bowl and whisk together with the salt, pepper and thyme. Toss the egg mixture gently with the potatoes, onions and chorizo.

Heat the vegetable oil in the skillet over high heat until it just begins to smoke. Pour the frittata mixture into the skillet and shake gently to evenly distribute the filling.

Place the skillet directly into the oven and bake for 25 to 30 minutes, until the frittata is puffed and golden. Cut into thick wedges and serve right out of the skillet with Picante Sauce on the side.

Mildred Says

Brown, white, small, jumbo, free-range, omega-3s – which came first? An egg's colour is decided by the breed of the hen. Eggs are graded by weight per dozen, from peewee to jumbo. Free-range eggs are generally sold directly from the farm and come from hens that are free to scratch and pick. Omega-3 eggs come from hens that are fed a controlled diet with increased amounts of "good" fatty acids. A dozen eggs, a dozen choices.

Ida's Famous French Toast

With "Ida's Gone Bananas" Compote

SERVES 4

Ida was one hard-working dame, on her feet at Mildred's diner from morning 'til night. She could juggle dinner plates and demanding guests with the best of them, but she knew that the real key to keeping customers happy were those special little touches. That's why she made her French toast with brioche, which gives this brunch classic an irresistible flavour, texture and richness. At Mildred Pierce Restaurant we serve it with "Ida's Gone Bananas" Compote. But try it with CPR Strawberries (see Mildred's Pantry, page 116) or a hefty pour of maple syrup.

"IDA'S GONE BANANAS" COMPOTE

1½ cups	375 mL	fresh squeezed orange juice
¼ cup	60 mL	fresh squeezed lemon juice
¼ cup	60 mL	maple syrup
2 T	30 mL	brown sugar, packed
¼ cup	60 mL	unsalted butter, cubed
2	2	ripe bananas, thinly sliced

In a stainless-steel saucepan, combine the orange and lemon juice and boil for 15 minutes. Reduce the heat to low and add the maple syrup and brown sugar, stirring until the sugar has dissolved. Keep warm. Just before serving, whisk in the butter and add the sliced bananas.

PUTTING IT ALL TOGETHER

7 large	7 large	eggs
1 cup	250 mL	35% cream
2 T	30 mL	maple syrup
pinch	pinch	ground nutmeg
¼ tsp	1 mL	ground cinnamon
1 loaf	1 loaf	Perfect Breakfast Brioche (see page 32)
½ cup	125 mL	unsalted butter

Preheat the oven to 350°F (180°C).

Whisk together the eggs, cream, maple syrup, nutmeg and cinnamon. Pour into a wide, shallow dish.

Using a serrated knife, trim the crusts from each end of the brioche and cut the loaf into 1" (2.5 cm) thick slices. Lay the slices into the egg mixture, turning over once to soak through.

Melt 2 T (30 mL) of the butter in a nonstick skillet over medium heat. Gently lift a few slices of brioche from the egg mixture and lay into the hot skillet (be careful not to overcrowd the skillet). Cook until golden, about 1 minute per side.

Transfer the slices to a baking sheet and bake in the oven for about 5 minutes, until puffed and set through. Arrange 2 slices of French toast on a warm plate and heap with "Ida's Gone Bananas" Compote and a dusting of Cinnamon Sugar (see page 36).

Mildred Says

Maple syrup comes in many grades – the most desirable being Grade A, which is light amber in colour and has a delicate, sweet taste. Once opened, pure maple syrup should be stored in the refrigerator, but it's best enjoyed at room temperature. Imitation "maple flavoured" syrup will not do.

Roasted Cherry Tomato Tart
With Goat's Milk Cheese and Arugula

SERVES 6 TO 8

The wonderful thing about this recipe is that you can use its proportion of cream to eggs with just about any filling and you'll end up with a perfect tart every time. Gruyère with Red Onion Marmalade (see Mildred's Pantry, page 110) or Stilton with leek will make fabulous alternatives.

ROASTED CHERRY TOMATOES

½ tsp	2 mL	kosher salt
pinch	pinch	cracked black pepper
½ tsp	2 mL	garlic, minced
1 tsp	5 mL	fresh marjoram, chopped
1 tsp	5 mL	fresh rosemary, chopped
1 T	15 mL	extra virgin olive oil
1 pint	500 mL	cherry tomatoes, halved

Preheat the oven to 350°F (180°C).

In a bowl, mix together the salt, pepper, garlic, marjoram, rosemary and olive oil. Add the cherry tomatoes and toss gently until evenly coated. Spread the tomatoes out in a single layer, cut side up, on a parchment paper–lined baking sheet. Roast for 12 to 15 minutes until tender.

PUTTING IT ALL TOGETHER

¾ lb	400 g	Five Star Pastry (see Mildred's Pantry, page 118)
½ cup	125 mL	Asiago cheese, grated
½ cup	125 mL	goat's milk cheese
1 cup	250 mL	Roasted Cherry Tomatoes
½ cup	125 mL	arugula, chiffonade
1 T	15 mL	fresh marjoram, chopped
4 large	4 large	eggs
2 cups	500 mL	35% cream
1 tsp	5 mL	kosher salt

Increase the oven temperature to 375°F (190°C).

On a lightly floured surface, roll the Five Star Pastry out into a 15" (38 cm) round, about 1/8" (3 mm) thick. Line an 11" (28 cm) fluted tart pan with a removable bottom with the pastry, trimming away any overhang. Refrigerate for at least 30 minutes.

Sprinkle the pastry shell with the Asiago cheese and crumble in the goat's milk cheese. Distribute the Roasted Cherry Tomatoes, arugula and marjoram evenly over the cheeses. Place the tart shell on a baking sheet.

In a small bowl, whisk together the eggs, cream and salt. Carefully pour the egg mixture into the tart shell to cover the filling. Jiggle the filling a little to make sure that the egg and cream mixture gets right down to the bottom of the tart.

Bake for 1 hour, until the tart is golden and the centre is almost set. Let cool for 10 minutes before removing the fluted ring. Serve the tart warm or at room temperature.

MILDRED SAYS

Some things slice up better when they're cold and some things taste better the next day. If refrigerated, the tart will cut into perfect wedges. Reheat the individual wedges in a 350°F (180°C) oven until warmed through. Try this helpful hint with Mildred's Apple Streusel Pie and our Mac and Cheese too.

Corned Beef Hash

With Fried Eggs and Pepper Rouille

SERVES 6

Corned beef hash, a Midwestern American favourite, is typically a "fry up" using leftovers from last night's supper. Ours is a delicious ragoût of tomatoes, peppers, onions, corned beef and crispy potatoes. We like to serve this dish with sunny-side eggs and zesty Pepper Rouille, but it's great on its own.

1 cup	250 mL	dried navy beans
3 T	45 mL	olive oil
1½ cups	375 mL	onions (about 1), finely diced
1 T	15 mL	garlic, minced
1 cup	250 mL	red pepper, diced
1 cup	250 mL	yellow pepper, diced
½ tsp	2 mL	paprika
½ tsp	2 mL	chili powder
½ tsp	2 mL	ground cumin
28 fl oz tin	796 mL tin	plum tomatoes
½ tsp	2 mL	Tabasco
1 tsp	5 mL	kosher salt
½ lb	227 g	corned beef, cut into ½" (12 mm) cubes
		vegetable oil for frying
1 lb	454 g	Yukon Gold potatoes, about 4 cups (1 L), cut into ½" (12 mm) cubes
¼ cup	60 mL	fresh oregano, chopped
¼ cup	60 mL	fresh Italian parsley, chopped
12 large	12 large	eggs, sunny-side up
1 recipe	1 recipe	Pepper Rouille (see Mildred's Pantry, page 111)

Soak the navy beans overnight in a large pot of cold water.

The next morning, drain and rinse the beans, then place them in a saucepan with 4 cups (1 L) of fresh cold water. Simmer for 45 minutes or until tender. Drain and set aside.

In a large saucepan, heat the olive oil over medium heat. Sauté the onions, garlic and peppers until soft, about 3 minutes. Add the paprika, chili powder and cumin and continue to cook for 2 more minutes.

Remove the saucepan from the heat. Strain the juice from the tinned tomatoes directly into the saucepan. Roughly chop the tomatoes and add them along with the Tabasco, salt, beans and corned beef. Simmer the hash for 15 minutes, stirring occasionally.

Meanwhile, heat 1/2" (12 mm) vegetable oil in a large skillet over high heat. When the oil is good and hot, add the cubed potatoes and fry for 7 to 10 minutes until crispy outside and tender inside. Using a slotted spoon or spider, remove the potatoes and place on paper towels to absorb any excess oil.

Stir the oregano and parsley into the hash and portion into warm bowls. Scatter the crispy potatoes over the hash and serve each with sunny-side eggs and a dollop of Pepper Rouille.

Mildred Says

When making mayonnaise-based sauces such as rouille or aïoli, it's important to add the oil in a slow, steady stream to ensure that the sauce comes together in a smooth, thick emulsion. This can be tricky when you're balancing a measuring cup of oil in one hand and whisking with the other. Put the oil in a plastic **squeeze bottle** so that you can easily control the stream.

Roasted Pepper and Basil Strata

SERVES 6

Strata is an Italian savoury bread pudding. It's commonly made with leftover daily bread, soaked with milk, eggs and herbs and baked until it puffs up like a soufflé. Delicious served with Roasted Cherry Tomatoes (see page 58) and a green salad.

BEFORE YOU START ...
The night before, remove all the crusts from the loaf and slice bread into 3/4" (2 cm) cubes. Spread the cubes out onto a baking sheet and leave out to dry overnight. The drier the bread, the better your results will be.

2 T	30 mL	unsalted butter
1 cup	250 mL	onion, thinly sliced
1 loaf	1 loaf	Perfect Breakfast Brioche (see page 32) or crusty Italian loaf, cubed and dried (about 10 cups/2.5 L)
½ cup	125 mL	feta cheese, crumbled
½ cup	125 mL	fontina cheese, grated
½ cup	125 mL	roasted red peppers, peeled, seeded and sliced
½ cup	125 mL	roasted yellow peppers, peeled, seeded and sliced
¼ cup	60 mL	fresh basil, chiffonade
5 large	5 large	eggs
1 cup	250 mL	2% milk
1½ tsp	7 mL	kosher salt
1 tsp	5 mL	dry mustard

Melt the butter in a skillet over medium heat. Add the onions and cook until soft and just beginning to brown, about 10 minutes.

In a large bowl, toss together the dry bread cubes with the onions, feta and fontina cheeses, roasted peppers and basil.

In a small bowl, whisk together the eggs, milk, salt and dry mustard. Pour the egg mixture over the bread cubes, gently tossing to combine.

Divide the bread mixture evenly into a buttered jumbo muffin tin (for 6 muffins). Cover lightly with plastic wrap and leave in the refrigerator for 30 minutes.

Meanwhile, preheat the oven to 350°F (180°C).

Remove the plastic wrap and place the muffin tin on a baking sheet. Bake the strata for 40 minutes until puffed and golden brown. Enjoy immediately.

MILDRED SAYS
You'll get the best texture from your strata if you make it with stale bread, which acts as a sponge to soak up all the tasty flavours. If your loaf is just too fresh (and time is of the essence), getting nice, even cubes for the strata can be a bit of a challenge. Here are two helpful tips. Try freezing the bread into cubes. To use the cubes the same day, spread them out on a baking sheet and dry in a 200°F (100°C) oven for 15 to 20 minutes.

The Manhandler
Steak and Eggs with Rosemary Roasted Potatoes
FEEDS 1 HUNGRY MAN

How do you handle a hungry man? With the Manhandler – a great big hearty meal of steak, fried eggs, roasted potatoes and our soon-to-be-famous MP Sauce. (Warning: May make you want to go outside and chop wood or herd cattle.)

ROSEMARY ROASTED POTATOES

1 lb	454 g	Yukon Gold potatoes, peeled and cut into 1" (2.5 cm) pieces
1 T	15 mL	unsalted butter, melted
1 T	15 mL	olive oil
1 T	15 mL	fresh rosemary, finely chopped
1 tsp	5 mL	kosher salt
1 tsp	5 mL	cracked black pepper

Preheat the oven to 400°F (200°C).

Place the potatoes in a large pot of cold, well-salted water and bring to a boil. Reduce the heat to medium and cook until potatoes are just tender, about 7 minutes. Drain the potatoes and let them steam-dry in the colander for 5 minutes.

Meanwhile, heat a baking sheet in the oven. Toss the warm potatoes with the melted butter, olive oil, rosemary, salt and pepper. Spread them out in a single layer on the hot baking sheet. Roast for 30 minutes, giving them a stir occasionally.

PUTTING IT ALL TOGETHER

1 T	15 mL	fresh rosemary, chopped
1 tsp	5 mL	garlic, minced
2 T	30 mL	balsamic vinegar
¼ cup	60 mL	olive oil
1 tsp	5 mL	cracked black pepper
1	1	8 oz (227 g) striploin steak
½ tsp	2 mL	kosher salt
2 large	2 large	eggs, sunny-side up

Combine the rosemary, garlic, balsamic vinegar, olive oil and pepper. Pour over the steak and marinate in the refrigerator for about an hour.

Preheat the oven to 400°F (200°C).

Remove the steak from the marinade. Season both sides of the steak with the salt.

Heat a skillet over high heat. Lay the steak into the skillet and sear each side for about 1 minute. Place the skillet directly into the oven. For a medium-rare steak cook for 5 minutes.

Remove the skillet from the oven. Let the steak rest on a cutting board for a couple of minutes before serving to let the juices settle.

Serve with 2 sunny-side eggs, our Rosemary Roasted Potatoes and MP Sauce (see Mildred's Pantry, page 115).

Mildred Says

The grill is the ideal way to cook a steak, but grilling is not always possible. As an alternative, we recommend a seasoned cast-iron skillet with an ovenproof handle. Heat the skillet over high heat. (Don't be afraid to let the skillet get really hot – this will prevent the steak from sticking and adds gorgeous flavour and colour.)

VEDA
You think new curtains are enough to make me happy?
No, I want more.
I want the kind of life that Monty taught me.

BIG BREAKFAST

For many people who love brunch, eggs are not enough. Which brings us to the heartier dishes we offer our guests. From our big stack of Mrs. Biederhof's Blueberry Buttermilk Pancakes to our opulent Lobster Pot Pie, these decadent Big Breakfasts are hearty enough to see you right through until dinner. Go ahead, spoil yourself. But remember to leave room for dessert.

Mrs. Biederhof's
Blueberry Buttermilk Pancakes

MAKES A STACK OF 12

We named these after Mrs. Biederhof, the notorious "other woman" vying for Mildred's husband's affections, because we like to imagine her luring Bert away with these rich, buttery pancakes. This recipe makes pancakes like none you've ever had. They're thick and fluffy, with fresh blueberries strewn throughout. The real trick to these is in the mixing. If you overmix the batter, the pancakes won't be moist and delicate – like Mrs. Biederhof's.

2 cups	500 mL	all-purpose flour
¼ cup	60 mL	white sugar
½ tsp	2 mL	salt
2¼ tsp	11 mL	baking powder
½ tsp	2 mL	baking soda
2 large	2 large	eggs
2 cups	500 mL	buttermilk
¼ cup	60 mL	unsalted butter, melted
1 cup	250 mL	fresh blueberries
		unsalted butter to grease the skillet

In a large bowl, sift together the flour, sugar, salt, baking powder and baking soda.

In a separate bowl, beat the eggs with the buttermilk and melted butter.

Using a spatula, combine the dry and wet ingredients to make a thick, lumpy batter, taking care not to overmix.

In a nonstick skillet, melt some butter over medium-high heat. Ladle 1/3 cup (75 mL) of batter into the hot skillet and sprinkle with blueberries. Take care not to overcrowd the skillet, since the pancakes will puff up as they cook.

When bubbles appear on the surface of the pancakes and the edges begin to brown, flip the pancakes and cook the other side. It should take about 2 to 3 minutes per side. If you're making these faster than you're eating them (which is highly unlikely), keep the pancakes warm in a 250°F (120°C) oven.

Smother with maple syrup and dollop with whipped cream.

MILDRED SAYS

You'll love these pancakes so much, don't be surprised if you crave them every day of the week. To help make this possible, here's a quick tip: Premeasure and mix all the dry ingredients together and store in ziplock bags. Then all you need to do is add the wet ingredients and heat up your skillet.

Chicken and Waffles

With Dijon Cream Sauce and Blueberry Green Peppercorn Chutney

SERVES 4

Mildred was famous for her chicken and waffles. Sound unusual? We thought so too, until we discovered a 1950's book of Southern cookery that included a recipe for chicken and waffles. We tried it and loved it! Hope you do too.

Before You Start...
If you don't own an electric waffle iron, skip this recipe. This is one piece of equipment you don't want to substitute.

WAFFLES

½ cup	125 mL	all-purpose flour
½ cup	125 mL	whole-wheat flour
1 tsp	5 mL	baking powder
½ tsp	2 mL	baking soda
½ tsp	2 mL	salt
1 T	15 mL	white sugar
1 T	15 mL	dry mustard
1 large	1 large	egg
½ cup	125 mL	buttermilk
½ cup	125 mL	unsalted butter, melted
1 T	15 mL	fresh thyme, finely chopped

Sift together the all-purpose and whole-wheat flour with the baking powder, baking soda, salt, sugar and dry mustard. In a small bowl, whisk together the egg, buttermilk and melted butter. Mix the wet ingredients into the dry ingredients and stir in the thyme. The batter is now ready to use. For best results, follow the cooking directions on your waffle iron.

PUTTING IT ALL TOGETHER

4	4	7 oz (200 g) boneless chicken breasts, skin on
1 T	15 mL	olive oil
1 tsp	5 mL	kosher salt
½ tsp	2 mL	cracked black pepper
1 recipe	1 recipe	Dijon Cream Sauce (see Mildred's Pantry, page 114)
1 recipe	1 recipe	Blueberry Green Peppercorn Chutney (see Mildred's Pantry, page 110)

Preheat the oven to 400°F (200°C).

Heat a large ovenproof skillet over medium-high heat. Rub the chicken breasts with olive oil, salt and pepper and place skin-side down in the hot skillet. Cook for 2 to 3 minutes until the skin is golden and crispy. Turn the breasts over and cook for another minute. Flip the chicken back onto the skin side and place the skillet directly in the oven. Roast for 10 to 12 minutes or until the juices run clear. Remove the skillet from the oven and let the chicken rest for several minutes before slicing.

Slice each chicken breast into three. Place the waffles on warm plates and arrange the chicken slices on top. Generously spoon warm Dijon Cream Sauce over the chicken and top with a heaping helping of Blueberry Green Peppercorn Chutney.

Chester Salmon Salad

SERVES 4

We generally stand by the adage "If it ain't broke, don't fix it," but our version of the classic Niçoise salad is a worthy recreation of this dish enlivened with Lemon Baked Salmon, blue potatoes, cherry tomatoes and a bold Saffron Aïoli.

BLUE POTATO SALAD

1 lb	454 g	blue potatoes, skins on, sliced into ¼" (6 mm) rounds
½ cup	125 mL	Lemon Vinaigrette (see Mildred's Pantry, page 108)
¼ lb	115 g	green beans, trimmed
2 sprigs	2 sprigs	fresh oregano
½ cup	125 mL	red onion, very thinly sliced
6	6	red cherry tomatoes, halved
6	6	yellow cherry tomatoes, halved
1	1	roasted red pepper, peeled, seeded and sliced into ¼" (6 mm) strips
1	1	roasted yellow pepper, peeled, seeded and sliced into ¼" (6 mm) strips
2 T	30 mL	capers
½ cup	125 mL	Niçoise olives
1 T	15 mL	kosher salt

Place the potatoes in a large pot of well-salted cold water. Add a splash of white vinegar, bring to a boil and cook for 1 minute. Remove the pot from the heat and let stand for 5 minutes. (This gentle cooking method helps to keep the potato slices intact.) Drain the potatoes and let steam-dry in a colander for 3 minutes. Gently toss the potatoes with 1/4 cup (60 mL) of the Lemon Vinaigrette.

Blanch the beans to maintain their brilliant green colour and crunchy bite. Pick the oregano leaves from the sprigs, discarding the stems. In a large bowl, combine the potatoes, beans, oregano, red onion, cherry tomatoes, roasted peppers, capers, olives and salt. Toss with the remaining Lemon Vinaigrette.

LEMON BAKED SALMON

4	4	5 oz (140 g) Atlantic salmon fillets, skin off
2 T	30 mL	olive oil
2 T	30 mL	fresh tarragon, chopped
1 T	15 mL	grated lemon zest
1 tsp	5 mL	kosher salt
1 tsp	5 mL	cracked black pepper

Preheat the oven to 400°F (200°C).

Place the salmon fillets 2" (5 cm) apart on a parchment paper–lined baking sheet. Drizzle the salmon with the olive oil and sprinkle with tarragon, lemon zest, salt and pepper. Bake for 10 to 12 minutes. For the best flavour and texture, the salmon should be pale pink on the outside and a deeper pink in the middle.

PUTTING IT ALL TOGETHER

1 recipe	1 recipe	Saffron Aïoli (see Mildred's Pantry, page 113)
½ cup	125 mL	Chive Oil (see Mildred's Pantry, page 108)

Arrange generous heapings of Blue Potato Salad onto 4 plates. Lay the Lemon Baked Salmon on top. Add a dollop of Saffron Aïoli and a drizzle of Chive Oil.

Mildred Says

Make friends with your fishmonger. When choosing fresh salmon, look for fish that is firm to the touch and has a deep red colour and a clean sea-sweet smell. Whenever possible, choose whole fish and have your fishmonger prepare the fillets for you.

The Wally

Grilled Focaccia with Roasted Peppers, Black Olive Pesto, Eggplant and Asiago

SERVES 6

This deluxe sandwich should be served hot, gooey and dripping with cheese. Make sure to choose a traditional, flat focaccia, not the big, doughy imposters that some stores sell. To save time and to intensify the flavours of these sandwiches, prepare them a day in advance and wrap them snugly in plastic wrap so that all the flavours blend together. The next day, simply grill and serve.

¼ cup	60 mL	all-purpose flour
¼ tsp	1 mL	kosher salt
½ tsp	2 mL	cracked black pepper
1 medium	1 medium	Italian eggplant, cut lengthwise into ¼" (6 mm) thick slices
1 cup	250 mL	olive oil
1	1	focaccia, about 10" x 6" (25 cm x 15 cm)
1 recipe	1 recipe	Black Olive Pesto (see Mildred's Pantry, page 112)
4	4	ripe tomatoes, thinly sliced
2	2	roasted red peppers, peeled and seeded
1½ cups	375 mL	Asiago cheese, grated

In a shallow dish (large enough to hold the eggplant slices), combine the flour, salt and pepper. Lightly coat each eggplant slice with the seasoned flour.

In a large skillet, heat 1/4 cup (60 mL) of the olive oil over medium-high heat. Fry the eggplant slices until golden brown on both sides, adding more oil as needed. (Be generous with the olive oil, as the eggplant slices are highly absorbent.) Remove the slices from the skillet and blot lightly on paper towel.

Cut the focaccia in half horizontally. Spread the inside of both halves with the Black Olive Pesto. On one half arrange the eggplant slices, layer the tomatoes and roasted peppers on top and sprinkle with Asiago cheese. Cover with the other focaccia half, pressing firmly to join. Cut the sandwich in two. Wrap each piece tightly in plastic wrap and refrigerate overnight (or at least a couple of hours) to bind the ingredients together.

Preheat the oven to 350°F (180°C).

Heat a large skillet over medium-high heat. Unwrap the sandwiches and brush each side of the focaccia with olive oil. Grill both sides until golden and crispy. Place the sandwiches on a baking sheet and into the oven for at least 10 minutes, or until the cheese is melted and gooey. Cut each sandwich into three and serve warm.

Mildred Says

Roasting peppers brings out their flavour and sweetness. To roast a pepper perfectly, place the whole pepper on a baking sheet in a 375°F (190°C) oven for 35 to 40 minutes until it's slightly charred and blistered. Carefully transfer the pepper to a small bowl and cover tightly with plastic wrap. The trapped steam will loosen the skin, making peeling easier. When the pepper is cool enough to handle, peel off the skin with your fingers and discard the seeds and stem.

Shrimp and Crab Cakes

SERVES 4

Mildred and Monty spent the first weekend of their torrid affair at Monty's swank beach house, steps from the ocean. Our divine Shrimp and Crab Cakes, made with luscious pieces of decadent seafood, are a tribute to their seaside romance. Ginger and kaffir lime combine to give these cakes their fresh, exotic taste, while jicama gives them a crisp texture. Our Asian Pear and Fennel Toss-Up (see page 78) is a perfect complement for these sensational cakes.

¾ lb	400 g	raw shrimp, peeled and deveined
2 large	2 large	egg whites
¼ cup	60 mL	35% cream
1½ tsp	7 mL	kosher salt
¼ tsp	1 mL	cracked black pepper
½ tsp	2 mL	cumin seeds
½ cup	125 mL	jicama, peeled and cut into ¼" (6 mm) cubes
3	3	green onions, white parts only, finely chopped
2 T	30 mL	fresh cilantro, chopped
1½ T	22 mL	ginger, finely grated
3	3	kaffir lime leaves, minced
¾ lb	400 g	crab meat
3 cups	750 mL	panko
		vegetable oil for frying

Chop the raw shrimp coarsely and place in a large bowl.

In a small bowl, whip the egg whites with a fork until frothy. Stir in the cream, salt, pepper and cumin seeds and mix into the chopped shrimp. Add the jicama, green onion, cilantro, ginger and kaffir lime, mixing well.

Press any excess moisture out of the crab meat. Combine the crab with the shrimp mixture.

Pour the panko into a wide, shallow dish. Using an ice cream scoop, scoop out about 1/4 cup (60 mL) of the shrimp and crab mixture and drop it into the dish. Using your hands, shape the shrimp and crab mixture into round cakes and evenly coat with panko. Place each crab cake on a parchment paper–lined baking sheet and refrigerate for 30 minutes until firm.

Heat a deep-fryer to 350°F (180°C) or heat 3/4" (2 cm) of vegetable oil in a skillet over medium heat just until the surface of the oil begins to gently ripple. Fry the crab cakes, a few at a time, until crispy and golden, about 2 minutes per side. Remove from the hot oil with a slotted spoon or spider and place on paper towels to absorb any excess oil.

These crab cakes are great served with our Saffron Aïoli (see Mildred's Pantry, page 113).

MILDRED SAYS

Ice cream scoops make ideal measures for scooping out perfectly round portions of cookie doughs and pancake and muffin batters. Choose a scoop with a quick-release handle. Grease the scoop with a little vegetable oil, and batters will slip out easily. Try this tip for portioning the shrimp and crab mixture into cakes.

Asian Pear and Fennel Toss-Up

SERVES 4

This fresh, crisp, citrusy salad has fantastic crunch. Great with our Shrimp and Crab Cakes and Lobster Pot Pie (see pages 76, 79) or on its own, dolled up with toasted pecans and crumbled Stilton.

¼ cup	60 mL	red onion, very thinly sliced
½ cup	125 mL	Asian pear, peeled and cut in ½" (12 mm) cubes
1 T	15 mL	fresh squeezed lemon juice
1 bunch	1 bunch	watercress
1½ cups	375 mL	fennel, thinly sliced
¾ cup	175 mL	celery root, peeled and cut into thin matchsticks
1	1	ruby red grapefruit, cut into segments
¼ cup	60 mL	Orange Vinaigrette (see Mildred's Pantry, page 108)
½ tsp	2 mL	kosher salt
½ tsp	2 mL	cracked black pepper

Soak the red onion slices in ice water to keep them crisp and to draw out any sharpness. Drain after 30 minutes.

Peel the Asian pear and cut into 1/2" (12 mm) cubes. To help maintain its colour, toss the pear with the lemon juice.

Remove any large, thick stems from the watercress.

Peel the celery root with a paring knife, cutting off any brown knobs. Slice the celery root into thin slices and then cut the slices into matchsticks.

In a large bowl, gently toss together the red onion, Asian pear, watercress, celery root, fennel and grapefruit segments.

Dress with the Orange Vinaigrette and season with salt and pepper.

MILDRED SAYS

A segment of citrus fruit should be free of peel and membrane. To segment, first slice the top and bottom off the fruit. Use a **serrated** paring knife to slice away the peel until you're right down to the flesh. Slice down to the core on each side of the segment, releasing it from the membrane. These skinless, seedless segments are perfect for salads when a juicy bite of fruit is desired.

Lobster Pot Pie

SERVES 8

There's pot pie, and then there's our ultra-extravagant Lobster Pot Pie made with an abundance of lobster, shrimp and scallops. We won't lie to you – this dish is a lot of work. But if you love seafood, it's just about the best work you can get.

1½ lbs	680 g	Five Star Pastry (see Mildred's Pantry, page 118)
¼ cup	60 mL	olive oil
1 T	15 mL	garlic, minced
¾ cup	175 mL	shallots, finely chopped
¾ cup	175 mL	leek, white part, cut in ½" (12 mm) cubes
¾ cup	175 mL	carrot, peeled and cut in ½" (12 mm) cubes
¾ cup	175 mL	celery, cut in ½" (12 mm) cubes
2 cups	500 mL	potatoes (about ½ lb/250 g), peeled and cut in ½" (12 mm) cubes
1½ cups	375 mL	white wine, dry Riesling
1½ cups	375 mL	35% cream
⅓ cup	75 mL	all-purpose flour
1 T	15 mL	fresh thyme, finely chopped
2 T	30 mL	fresh Italian parsley, finely chopped
1 T	15 mL	fresh tarragon, chopped
1 lb	454 g	raw shrimp, peeled and deveined
1 lb	454 g	raw sea scallops, whole
1½ lbs	680 g	raw lobster meat, cut into large pieces
1 T	15 mL	kosher salt
1 tsp	5 mL	cracked black pepper
1 large	1 large	egg
1 T	15 mL	grainy Dijon mustard

Divide the pastry in half. On a lightly floured surface, roll out two 16" (40 cm) circles about 1/4" (6 mm) thick. Line an oval casserole dish 10" x 2" (25 cm x 5 cm) with one pastry circle, leaving about a 1" (2.5 cm) overhang. Lay the second circle out on a parchment paper–lined baking sheet. Refrigerate both circles.

Preheat the oven to 425°F (220°F). Heat the olive oil in a large saucepan over medium heat. Sauté the garlic, shallots and leeks for about 2 minutes. Add the carrots, celery and potatoes, cooking until the vegetables are soft, about 5 more minutes. Add the wine and cook for another 3 minutes, stirring occasionally. Pour the cream into a small bowl, sprinkle the surface with flour and whisk to combine. Stir this mixture into the pot of vegetables. Cook over medium heat, stirring constantly until very thick. Remove the pot from the heat and cool to room temperature. (This is a crucial step. If you add in all that beautiful seafood while the mixture is still hot, it will overcook.) Once the mixture has cooled completely, fold in the fresh herbs, seafood, salt and pepper. Pour into the prepared casserole and distribute the filling evenly. Whisk together the egg and mustard and brush it on the overhanging pastry. Cover the pie with the pastry top and seal the edges together. Trim away any excess pastry and decoratively crimp the edges. Brush the top of the pie with the remaining egg wash and make three 2" (5 cm) long cuts in the top to allow steam to escape.

Bake at 425°F (220°C) for 15 minutes, then turn the heat down to 350°F (180°C) and bake for 20 to 25 minutes more. Let stand for 15 minutes before serving.

Mildred Says

Our Five Star Pastry works equally well for both sweet and savoury dishes. However, if you want to add a new spin to an old favourite, try this one.

Simply add 1 tsp (5 mL) of dry mustard and 1 T (15 mL) of finely chopped rosemary to the sifted flour in the Five Star Pastry and finish the recipe as directed. It's an outstanding complement to our Lobster Pot Pie or our Roasted Cherry Tomato Tart (see page 58).

Sunday Best Mac and Cheese

SERVES 6

This is mac and cheese dressed up in its Sunday best. Smoked chicken, Emmenthal and Cheesy Parmesan Sauce are baked with penne pasta to create this delectable comfort food. You could bake this dish the night before to give it time to set. The next day slice it like a pie, warm it up and serve with our Roasted Cherry Tomatoes.

2 T	30 mL	unsalted butter
2 cups	500 mL	onions (about 2), finely chopped
1 lb	454 g	dried penne pasta
1 recipe	1 recipe	Cheesy Parmesan Sauce (see Mildred's Pantry, page 115)
4 ½ cups	1.125 L	smoked chicken, shredded, about 1 whole chicken
2 cups	500 mL	Emmenthal cheese, grated
2 T	30 mL	fresh basil, chiffonade
2 T	30 mL	fresh marjoram, chopped
2 T	30 mL	fresh thyme, chopped
12 cloves	12 cloves	roasted garlic, chopped
2 tsp	10 mL	kosher salt
½ cup	125 mL	breadcrumbs

Preheat the oven to 375°F (190°C).

Butter a casserole dish or a springform pan 9" (23 cm) round x 3" (7.5 cm) deep.

In a saucepan, melt the butter over medium heat. Add the onions and sauté, stirring occasionally, until golden.

In a large pot of boiling salted water, cook the pasta until tender. Drain and let the pasta steam-dry in a colander for 2 minutes.

In a large bowl, combine the warm pasta with the Cheesy Parmesan Sauce, onions, smoked chicken, Emmenthal, fresh herbs, roasted garlic and salt. Mix well until all the ingredients are thoroughly combined.

Press the pasta mixture firmly into the prepared springform pan. Place the pan on a baking sheet. Sprinkle the top of the pasta with the breadcrumbs.

Bake for 35 to 40 minutes.

Remove the springform pan from the oven and let the pasta rest for at least 15 minutes. To remove, run a paring knife around the inside of the pan before releasing it. Cut the Mac and Cheese into wedges and serve with our Roasted Cherry Tomatoes (see page 58) and a green salad.

MILDRED SAYS

Roasting garlic sweetens and mellows the flavour. It's a great addition to mashed potatoes, savoury tarts, gravies and sauces. Normally you'd roast the entire bulb, but this can be a messy job when removing the roasted garlic from the skins. We suggest using peeled garlic cloves and wrapping them in a piece of aluminum foil. Roast in a 375°F (190°C) oven for 20 to 30 minutes (or until the garlic is very soft). This keeps it moist and makes it easier to work with.

MILDRED
Let's see now, we have a dozen peach, a dozen berry, a dozen pumpkin, a dozen cherry.
And after we finish the apple, we can quit for the night.

LOTTIE
I don't know how you keep it up, Mrs. Pierce. Honest, I don't. Now, I sleep all morning but you go down to that restaurant
and work and work just like you been sleeping all night, only you ain't.

MILDRED
It keeps me thin.

"LET'S NOT GET STICKY ABOUT IT"

Who decided there would be no dessert with breakfast? Fortunately, this rule does not apply at brunch. Our guests will tell you that there's always room for a New York Pecan Square after a stack of Blueberry Buttermilk Pancakes. And nothing rounds off Huevos Monty like our Ice Cream Profiteroles. We've assembled a star-studded cast of dessert recipes for the grand finale.

Ice Cream Profiteroles
With Dark Chocolate Sauce and Apple Jack Caramel
MAKES A LOT MORE THAN 6 PEOPLE SHOULD EAT

We estimate that we've made over 2 million profiteroles since we opened Mildred Pierce Restaurant. We usually serve three to a plate, but maybe we're just being stingy.

PÂTE À CHOUX

½ cup	125 mL	unsalted butter, cubed
1 cup	250 mL	water
2 T	30 mL	white sugar
pinch	pinch	salt
1⅓ cups	325 mL	all-purpose flour
6 large	6 large	eggs

Preheat the oven to 425°F (220°C).

Place the butter, water, sugar and salt in a saucepan and bring to a boil. When the butter has melted, remove from the heat and add the flour in all at once. Beat vigorously with a wooden spoon until the mixture pulls away from the sides of the saucepan and forms a ball. Over medium heat, continue to beat until a thin film forms on the bottom of the saucepan, indicating that the flour is cooked.

Transfer the ball of dough to an electric stand mixer fitted with a paddle attachment. Add the eggs in, one at a time, beating for 1 minute on medium speed after each addition. When all the eggs have been added, beat the mixture on high speed until smooth and glossy. (The delightful thing about this recipe is that you can never overmix it.)

Transfer the batter to a piping bag fitted with a 1/2" (12 mm) round piping tip. (Piping will be easier if the bag is filled only halfway.) Dab some batter on the 4 corners of a baking sheet and stick a sheet of parchment paper over top to prevent the sheet from lifting up as you pipe.

With the piping bag at a 90-degree angle to the baking sheet and the tip almost touching the parchment paper, gently squeeze out a mound of batter about 1" (2.5 cm) round. Pipe the mounds about 2" (5 cm) apart. Use a dampened finger to smooth down the top of the mounds.

Bake at 425°F (220°C) for 15 minutes on the middle rack of the oven. Reduce the heat to 350°F (180°C) and bake for another 10 minutes. Turn off the heat, and with the oven door ajar, leave the profiteroles in to crisp for 15 minutes.

PUTTING IT ALL TOGETHER

big ol' tub	1 tub	your favourite ice cream (see your freezer)
1 recipe	1 recipe	Dark Chocolate Sauce (see Mildred's Pantry, page 116)
1 recipe	1 recipe	Apple Jack Caramel (see Mildred's Pantry, page 116)

Slice each profiterole in half and sandwich with a scoop of your favourite ice cream. Pour on Dark Chocolate Sauce and drizzle with Apple Jack Caramel.

Mildred Says

Ice cream that comes directly from the freezer is not only difficult to scoop but is really too cold to taste all the flavours. To ensure that your ice cream is soft, creamy and full of flavour, take it from the freezer and put it in the refrigerator 15 minutes before serving.

Mildred's Apple Streusel Pie

MAKES 1 PIE

When Bert left Mildred, she didn't fret. Well, not for long, anyway. Instead, she baked a pie, and then another, and then another ... It wasn't long before Mildred's pies became famous. In her honour, we've created this recipe. The Royal Gala is our apple of choice – it has the perfect texture and just enough sweetness. Serve up a warm slice of Mildred's pie with a big scoop of vanilla ice cream.

CINNAMON STREUSEL

¼ cup	60 mL	white sugar
1 tsp	5 mL	ground cinnamon
1 cup	250 mL	all-purpose flour
6 T	90 mL	unsalted butter, cold

In a bowl, combine the sugar, cinnamon and flour. With your fingertips, crumble the butter into the mixture until it resembles cornmeal.

PUTTING IT ALL TOGETHER

10 oz	283 g	Five Star Pastry (see Mildred's Pantry, page 118)
7 cups	1.75 L	Royal Gala apples (about 7), peeled, cored and cut into ¼" (6 mm) slices
½ cup	125 mL	white sugar
¼ tsp	1 mL	grated nutmeg
pinch	pinch	salt
2 tsp	10 mL	grated lemon zest
2 T	30 mL	unsalted butter, cold
1 recipe	1 recipe	Cinnamon Streusel

On a lightly floured surface, roll the pastry out into a circle about 13" (32.5 cm) in diameter and 1/4" (6 mm) thick. Line a 9" (23 cm) pie plate with the pastry. Trim away the excess and decoratively crimp the edge. Refrigerate the pie shell for at least 30 minutes.

Preheat the oven to 375°F (190°C).

Meanwhile, toss the apples with the sugar, nutmeg, salt and lemon zest. Distribute the apples evenly into the pie shell. Dab the top with pieces of cold butter.

Pick up a handful of Cinnamon Streusel and press it together to form a big clump. Break off large pieces and crumble the streusel evenly over the apples.

Place the pie on a baking sheet and bake for 1 hour and 15 minutes.

Mildred Says

Wondering what to do with your bits of leftover pastry? Pull them together into a ball and roll out into a square about 1/8" (6 mm) thick. Brush the edges with a little cream and sprinkle the surface with Cinnamon Sugar (see page 36). Roll up the pastry into a tight log. Refrigerate for 15 to 20 minutes. Slice the log into rounds, about 1" (2.5 cm) thick, and place them on a baking sheet, sealed edge down. Bake these tasty treats in a 350°F (180°C) oven for 15 to 20 minutes.

Velvet Chocolate Brownies

MAKES A DOZEN

These brownies go over the top with the addition of mascarpone (a buttery-rich Italian triple-cream cheese), dark chocolate and a decadent layer of ganache. At Mildred Pierce Restaurant we cut them out in rounds so that there are always lots of snippets left for the staff to nibble on.

BROWNIES

1 cup	250 mL	unsalted butter
3 oz	90 g	best-quality semi-sweet chocolate, finely chopped
½ cup	125 mL	best-quality cocoa powder
1 cup	250 mL	white sugar
3 large	3 large	eggs
2 tsp	10 mL	vanilla extract
⅓ cup	75 mL	mascarpone cheese, soft
½ cup	125 mL	all-purpose flour
¼ tsp	1 mL	salt

Preheat the oven to 325°F (160°C). Butter a baking pan 7" x 7" (18 cm x 18 cm).

In a small saucepan, melt the butter and bring to a boil.

Place the chopped chocolate in a large bowl, pour in the hot butter and stir until completely melted. Sift in the cocoa and sugar, then beat in the eggs, vanilla and mascarpone, mixing until the batter is smooth. Gently fold the flour and salt into the batter.

Pour the batter into the prepared baking pan and spread evenly. Bake for 50 to 55 minutes, until springy to the touch. Let the brownie cool for 10 minutes, then invert onto a wire cooling rack and let cool completely.

GANACHE

6 T	90 mL	35% cream
3 T	45 mL	unsalted butter
6 oz	170 g	best-quality semi-sweet chocolate, finely chopped

Heat the cream, butter and chocolate in a small saucepan over low heat. Stir constantly until the chocolate has melted and the mixture is smooth.

Spread the warm ganache over the brownie. Wait until the ganache sets before cutting into squares.

Caramel Crème Brûlée

MAKES 6

How smooth is this ...? If these were stockings they'd be French, silky and have seams running up the back. This sensual fusion of sweet custard and crackly caramel is a Mildred Pierce favourite.

Before You Start ...
For this recipe you'll need 6 ramekins with a 1/2 cup (125 mL) capacity and 1 baking pan large enough to hold them, about 3" (7.5 cm) deep. A hand-held blowtorch is best to brûlée the tops.

3 cups	750 mL	35% cream
½ cup	125 mL	white sugar
2 T	30 mL	water
6 large	6 large	egg yolks
		some white sugar to brûlée tops

Preheat the oven to 325°F (160°C).

Heat the cream in a saucepan just until it begins to boil. Remove from the heat and keep warm.

Combine the sugar and water in a large saucepan. Boil until the mixture turns light amber in colour, about 7 minutes. (Keep a close watch – the sugar colours quickly, and if it becomes too dark it will taste bitter.)

At arm's length, slowly stir in the warm cream, being mindful of the steam and the possibility of the hot caramel cream bubbling over.

In a large bowl, whisk the egg yolks with a small amount of the hot caramel cream. (This will prevent the yolks from curdling.) Add the rest of the cream in a slow stream, whisking steadily until combined.

Strain the mixture through a fine sieve. Pour evenly among the 6 ramekins, and place the ramekins in the shallow baking pan.

Bring a full kettle of water to a boil. Carefully pour the boiling water from the kettle into the pan so that the water comes 2/3 of the way up the sides of the ramekins. (Take care not to splash water into the custards.) Cover the pan with a sheet of parchment paper. Carefully transfer the pan to the top rack of the oven. Bake for 45 to 50 minutes or until the centres of the custards are slightly jiggly and just barely set. The custards will set further as they cool.

Remove the ramekins from their water bath and refrigerate them until completely cool, about 1 hour.

Using a hand-held blowtorch, brûlée the custards just before serving. First, sprinkle each custard with 1 tsp (5 mL) of sugar. Tilt and tap the ramekin to spread the sugar evenly across the surface of the custard. Light the blowtorch and pass the tip of the flame over the sugar until it melts and begins to caramelize. A proper crème brûlée should have a thin, crackly crust of amber caramelized sugar.

Mildred Says
When your recipe calls for separating a large quantity of eggs, instead of juggling the yolk back and forth between the ragged shells to remove the white (which tends to break the yolk), try this instead: First, crack all the eggs into a large bowl and, using your hand, scoop out the egg yolks, one at a time, letting the whites slide through your fingers.

Strawberry Shortcakes

SERVES 8

Strawberry shortcake is a down-home dessert – a great way to enjoy summer's sweet berries. To mix it up a bit, try these light biscuits layered with Brown Sugar Cream and raspberries, blackberries or peaches soaked in your favourite liqueur.

STRAWBERRY COMPOTE

2 T	30 mL	white sugar
1 T	15 mL	framboise liqueur
1 qt	1 L	fresh strawberries, hulled and quartered

In a large bowl, combine the sugar, framboise and strawberries. Let stand for 30 minutes so that the strawberries will release their juices.

SHORTCAKES

2¼ cups	560 mL	all-purpose flour
4 tsp	20 mL	baking powder
½ tsp	2 mL	salt
2 T	30 mL	white sugar
¼ cup	60 mL	unsalted butter, cold
¾ cup	175 mL	2% milk
2 T	30 mL	water

Preheat the oven to 450°F (230°C).

In a large bowl, mix together the flour, baking powder, salt and sugar. Using a coarse cheese grater, grate the cold butter into the dry ingredients. With your fingertips, combine until the mixture is crumbly. In a saucepan, over low heat, gently warm the milk and water.

Make a well in the centre of the dry ingredients and pour in the warm liquid. With a fork, mix lightly just until the dough comes together.

On a lightly floured surface, gently knead the dough for about 30 seconds. Roll out to a 1" (2.5 cm) thickness and stamp out the shortcakes with a 3" (7.5 cm) cutter. Place 2" (5 cm) apart on a parchment paper–lined baking sheet. Bake for 10 to 12 minutes.

BROWN SUGAR CREAM

½ cup	125 mL	soft deli-style cream cheese
¼ cup	60 mL	brown sugar, packed
1 cup	250 mL	35% cream
1 tsp	5 mL	vanilla extract

In an electric stand mixer fitted with the whisk attachment, cream together the cream cheese and sugar until smooth and fluffy. Scrape down the sides of the mixer with a spatula. With the mixer running on low speed, slowly pour in the 35% cream. Add the vanilla extract and whip for 2 more minutes.

PUTTING IT ALL TOGETHER

Pull apart a warm shortcake. Place the bottom on a plate. Spoon some strawberry compote over top and cover with a whack of Brown Sugar Cream. Replace the top, and if you like, dust with icing sugar.

New York Pecan Squares

MAKES A DOZEN

These rich and buttery squares, made with pastry that's almost like a shortbread cookie, are a dream come true for anyone with a sweet tooth. At Mildred Pierce Restaurant we cut them big, serve them warm and top them with whipped cream and a dusting of icing sugar.

SHORTBREAD PASTRY

½ cup	125 mL	unsalted butter, soft
⅔ cup	150 mL	white sugar
2 cups	500 mL	pastry flour
½ tsp	2 mL	salt
1 large	1 large	egg
1 large	1 large	egg yolk

Preheat the oven to 400°F (200°C).

In a bowl, cream together the butter and sugar. Mix in the pastry flour and salt. Add the egg and yolk and mix thoroughly.

Press the pastry into the bottom of a baking pan 9" x 11" x 2" (23 cm x 28 cm x 5 cm). Refrigerate for at least 15 minutes.

Lay down a sheet of parchment paper on top of the chilled pastry and cover with 2 cups (1 L) of pie weights.

Blind-bake the pastry for 20 minutes. Cool completely before removing the pie weights and parchment paper.

PUTTING IT ALL TOGETHER

1 cup	250 mL	unsalted butter
1½ cups	375 mL	brown sugar, packed
¼ cup	60 mL	white sugar
½ cup	125 mL	honey
⅓ cup	75 mL	35% cream
4½ cups	1.125 L	pecan halves
¼ tsp	1 mL	salt

Reduce the oven temperature to 375°F (190°C).

While the pastry is cooling, combine the butter, brown sugar, white sugar, honey and salt in a large saucepan. Place over high heat and boil for 6 minutes. Remove from the heat and, at arm's length, carefully stir in the cream, being mindful of splatters. Add the pecans and mix thoroughly.

Pour the filling evenly over the cooled shortbread pastry. Bake for 20 minutes.

Allow to cool completely before cutting into squares.

Double-Crossed Biscotti

MAKES 1½ DOZEN

In the film, Mildred gets double-crossed twice – once by Wally and once by Monty. Maybe these tasty biscotti would have made her feel better.

⅔ cup	150 mL	white sugar
1½ cups	375 mL	all-purpose flour
¼ tsp	1 mL	salt
¼ cup	60 mL	cornmeal
½ tsp	2 mL	baking powder
⅓ cup	75 mL	unsalted butter, soft
¼ cup	60 mL	whole blanched almonds, toasted and chopped
¼ cup	60 mL	pine nuts, toasted
2 large	2 large	eggs
2 T	30 mL	Amaretto liqueur
¼ tsp	1 mL	almond extract

Preheat the oven to 350°F (180°C).

In a mixing bowl, combine the sugar, flour, salt, cornmeal and baking powder. Using your fingertips, work the butter into the dry ingredients until the texture resembles breadcrumbs. Add the almonds and pine nuts.

Whisk together the eggs, Amaretto and almond extract, and add to the dry ingredients. Mix until the dough comes together to form a ball.

Turn the dough out onto a parchment paper–lined baking sheet and form into a log about 12" (30 cm) long. Flatten the log slightly until it's approximately 1" (2.5 cm) thick and 3" (7.5 cm) wide. Bake for 40 to 45 minutes. Remove from the oven and let cool for 10 minutes.

Turn the heat down to 300°F (150°C).

Place the log on a cutting board, and using a serrated knife, cut 1/2" (12 mm) thick biscotti. Lay the biscotti flat on the baking sheet. Bake for 15 minutes, turn the biscotti over and bake for 15 minutes more.

Try dipping these crisp biscuits into our White Hot Mocha (see page 20).

Mildred Says

Toasting nuts brings out their natural flavour and crunch. Spread the nuts in a single layer on a baking sheet and toast in a 350°F (180°C) oven for about 7 to 10 minutes (depending on your nuts), giving them a shake about halfway through.

Snappy Ginger Cookies

MAKES 4 DOZEN

Inspired by a basic gingersnap recipe we found in an old cookbook, we've amped up these cookies by adding ground espresso and blackstrap molasses, which gives them a rich, intense flavour. They're crispy and spicy and will make you feel warm all over.

⅔ cup	150 mL	unsalted butter, soft
¼ cup	60 mL	brown sugar, packed
½ cup	125 mL	white sugar
1 large	1 large	egg yolk
2 T	30 mL	blackstrap molasses
1 cup	250 mL	all-purpose flour
½ tsp	2 mL	baking soda
1½ tsp	7 mL	ground ginger
1 tsp	5 mL	ground cinnamon
½ tsp	2 mL	ground cloves
½ tsp	2 mL	ground allspice
1 T	15 mL	ground espresso
¼ tsp	1 mL	salt
		white sugar for topping

Preheat the oven to 350°F (180°C).

In a bowl, cream together the butter, brown sugar and white sugar until light and fluffy. Add the egg yolk and molasses and mix well.

In a separate bowl, combine the flour, baking soda, ginger, cinnamon, cloves, allspice, espresso and salt. Mix the dry ingredients into the butter mixture. The dough will be very soft, so refrigerate it for at least 30 minutes to make it easier to work with.

Roll the chilled dough into tight 1" (2.5 cm) round logs, wrap snugly in plastic wrap, and chill until firm. (At this point the dough can be stored in the freezer. From the freezer, let stand at room temperature for 10 minutes before slicing.)

Unwrap the dough and slice into rounds 1/4" (6 mm) thick. Pour some white sugar into a shallow dish. Press the top of each cookie into the sugar and then place cookies sugar-side up on a parchment paper–lined baking sheet about 2" (5 cm) apart. Bake for 12 to 15 minutes. Leave the cookies on the baking sheet to cool for 5 minutes, then transfer them to a wire cooling rack. To make these cookies snappy, let cool completely.

Mildred Says

If you find that your oven is temperamental and your cookies are browning too much, try doubling up on the baking sheets. Spread a few pie weights out on a baking sheet, then place a second sheet on top. This will create a protective layer of air and will make your cookies (and other baked goods) perfect every time.

Chocolate and Cranberry Oatmeal Cookies

MAKES 2½ DOZEN

There's nothing like a chocolate cookie served warm and gooey from the oven. Instead of using chocolate chips, we chop our chocolate by hand to ensure that there's a big chunk of heavenly chocolate in each bite. Oh yeah, and there are cranberries in there, too.

½ cup	125 mL	unsalted butter, soft
¼ cup	60 mL	brown sugar, packed
½ cup	125 mL	white sugar
1 large	1 large	egg
½ tsp	2 mL	vanilla extract
¾ cup	175 mL	all-purpose flour
½ tsp	2 mL	salt
½ tsp	2 mL	baking soda
2 tsp	10 mL	hot water
3 oz	90 g	best-quality chocolate, chopped into ½" (12 mm) pieces
½ cup	125 mL	dried cranberries
1½ cups	375 mL	old-fashioned rolled oats

Preheat the oven to 350°F (180°C).

In a bowl, cream together the butter, brown sugar and white sugar until light and fluffy. Add the egg and vanilla and mix well.

In a separate bowl, sift together the flour, salt and baking soda and stir into the butter mixture. Add the hot water and stir to combine. Mix in the chocolate, cranberries and rolled oats.

For perfect, evenly shaped cookies, use a small ice cream scoop to drop the dough onto a parchment paper–lined baking sheet. Space the cookies about 2" (5 cm) apart and bake for 10 to 12 minutes. Cool for 5 minutes before removing from the baking sheet.

MILDRED
I was always in the kitchen.
I felt as though I'd been born in a kitchen and lived there all my life.
Except for the few hours it took to get married.

MILDRED'S PANTRY

Have you ever wondered how some cooks can whip up a feast in a flash? Their secret is a well-stocked cupboard. Here's a peek into our pantry – homemade jams, jellies and flavoured butters to spread on warm, delicious breads; spicy condiments that'll spark up any sandwich; citrusy vinaigrettes to perk up your greens; and decadent sauces to add a sweet finish.

Spread on Toast

Cranberry Pear Jam

MAKES 4 CUPS (1 L)

In the fall it's cranberries and pears – you'll love this warm, festive jam.

2 cups	500 mL	fresh cranberries
1 cup	250 mL	Bartlett pears, peeled, cored and chopped into ¼" (6 mm) cubes
1 pouch	85 mL	liquid pectin
1	1	orange, zested and segmented
1 cup	250 mL	fresh squeezed orange juice
4 cups	1 L	white sugar

In a large, stainless-steel pot, combine the cranberries, pears, pectin, orange zest, segments and juice. Bring to a boil, stirring constantly. Add the sugar and stir until completely dissolved. Bring back to a full boil and boil for 2 more minutes. Remove from the heat and skim the foam from the top of the jam.

Allow to cool slightly and then pour into prepared jars.

Peach and Amaretto Jam

MAKES 5 CUPS (1.25 L)

There's no added pectin in this recipe, so don't worry that it's not as firm as most jams. Great with our Best Buttermilk Biscuits (see page 26).

3 cups	750 mL	white sugar
5 cups	1.25 L	ripe freestone peaches (about 6), peeled, pitted and chopped into ½" (12 mm) cubes
½ cup	125 mL	fresh squeezed lemon juice
½ cup	125 mL	Amaretto liqueur

In a large stainless-steel pot, combine the sugar, peaches and lemon juice. Bring to a boil, stirring constantly to prevent the fruit from floating on the surface. Simmer for 10 minutes, skimming away any foam from the surface. Add the Amaretto and bring back to a boil, then reduce heat to medium and simmer for 5 more minutes.

Can be stored in the refrigerator or freezer.

Red Pepper Jelly

MAKES 5 CUPS (1.25 L)

We like to make a big batch of this ruby jelly in the fall, when red peppers are ripe and plentiful.

4 cups	1 L	red pepper (about 4), seeded and chopped
5½ cups	1.375 L	white sugar
1 cup	250 mL	white vinegar
⅓ cup	75 mL	fresh squeezed lemon juice
1 pouch	85 mL	liquid pectin

Place the red peppers in a food processor and process to a purée. Combine the peppers, sugar and vinegar in a large stainless-steel pot. Bring to a boil, stirring constantly to avoid scorching. Remove the pot from the heat and cool the jelly for 15 minutes. (This allows the peppers to cook slowly in the residual heat and prevents them from floating on the surface.) Add the lemon juice and pectin, then return to medium heat and simmer for 20 minutes more, stirring occasionally. Skim any foam that appears on the surface of the jelly.

Store in prepared jars.

Tomato Butter

MAKES 1½ CUPS (375 ML)

Melted over grilled fish or spread on toast to dip into soft-boiled eggs, this savoury butter is bursting with flavour.

1 T	15 mL	olive oil
1 tsp	5 mL	garlic, minced
2 T	30 mL	shallots, minced
1 cup	250 mL	Roma tomatoes (about 2), diced
¼ cup	60 mL	sun-dried tomatoes
¼ cup	60 mL	water
¾ cup	175 mL	unsalted butter, soft
1 T	15 mL	fresh marjoram, chopped
1 T	15 mL	fresh Italian parsley, chopped

Heat the olive oil in a saucepan over medium heat. Add the garlic and shallots and sauté until soft, about 2 minutes. Add the Roma tomatoes, sun-dried tomatoes and water. Reduce the heat to low and simmer for 10 minutes until thickened. Remove the saucepan from the heat and let the tomato mixture cool completely. In a food processor, purée the tomato mixture until smooth. Then add the butter and purée until just combined. Transfer the butter to a small bowl and fold in the marjoram and parsley.

Can be stored in a tightly sealed container in the refrigerator for up to 5 days or frozen for up to 2 months. Always serve the tomato butter at room temperature.

Strawberry Fruit Butter

MAKES 3 CUPS (750 ML)

Ripe strawberries provide just the right amount of natural sugar and juice for this sweet butter, but you can use almost any fruit that's in season.

1 cup	250 mL	ripe strawberries, hulled and cut into small pieces
1 T	15 mL	white sugar
1 lb	454 g	unsalted butter, soft
5 T	75 mL	icing sugar

In a bowl, combine the strawberries with the white sugar and let stand for 10 minutes until the berries have released their juices. In a separate bowl, using a wooden spoon, cream the butter and icing sugar until light and fluffy. Beat in the strawberries and their juices until evenly blended.

Can be stored in a covered container in the refrigerator for up to 5 days or frozen for up to 2 months. Always serve the strawberry butter at room temperature.

Apple Cardamom Butter

MAKES 3 CUPS (750 ML)

Fruit butter is fabulous on our Irish Soda Bread, oatmeal or on thick slices of cinnamon toast. Make plenty in the fall to keep handy throughout the winter.

4 lbs	1.8 kg	Granny Smith apples (about 10), peeled, cored and cut into 1" (2.5 cm) cubes
1½ cups	375 mL	apple cider
½ cup	125 mL	brown sugar, packed
1 T	15 mL	fresh squeezed lemon juice
½ tsp	2 mL	ground cardamom
2	2	cinnamon sticks

In a large stainless-steel pot, combine the apples, cider, brown sugar, lemon juice, cardamom and cinnamon sticks. Stir the mixture over high heat so that the apples release their juices. Reduce the heat to medium and simmer for 10 minutes, until the apples are soft. Remove the cinnamon sticks and discard. Let the mixture cool slightly. In a food processor, purée the apple mixture in batches until smooth. Return the apple purée to the pot, cover with a lid and cook over low heat until thickened, about 30 minutes. Stir occasionally to prevent scorching. Cool completely.

Can be stored in tightly covered containers in the fridge for several weeks.

Chocolate Pecan Smother

MAKES 2 CUPS (500 ML)

An entirely satisfying remedy for late-morning chocolate cravings – spread on toasted brioche, layer between crêpes or dip with fresh strawberries.

3 cups	750 mL	pecan halves
½ cup	125 mL	icing sugar
¼ cup	60 mL	best-quality cocoa powder
¼ cup	60 mL	vegetable oil
¼ cup	60 mL	powdered milk
1 tsp	5 mL	vanilla extract
1 T	15 mL	water

Preheat the oven to 325°F (160°C).

Place the pecans on a baking sheet and toast in the oven for 15 minutes. Let the pecans cool slightly. In a food processor, pulse the pecans with the icing sugar and cocoa until fine, about 2 minutes. While the processor is still running, add the vegetable oil and purée until the mixture is smooth. Combine the powdered milk, vanilla and water in a small bowl. Add to the pecan mixture and process for 3 minutes until well combined.

Can be stored in a tightly covered container for several months.

Get Friendly with Your Greens

Orange Vinaigrette

MAKES 1¾ CUPS (425 ML)

This citrusy vinaigrette is great on our Asian Pear and Fennel Toss-Up (see page 78), but also try it tossed with spinach greens or warm beets.

¼ cup	60 mL	fresh squeezed orange juice
¼ cup	60 mL	rice vinegar
¼ cup	60 mL	white wine vinegar
½ cup	125 mL	olive oil
½ cup	125 mL	extra virgin olive oil
1 tsp	5 mL	orange oil
1 tsp	5 mL	kosher salt

In a small bowl, whisk together the orange juice, rice vinegar and white wine vinegar. Slowly drizzle in the olive oil and extra virgin olive oil, whisking continuously to emulsify. Mix in the orange oil and salt.

Can be stored in a jar in the refrigerator for up to 1 week. Give it a good shake before using.

Lemon Vinaigrette

MAKES 1½ CUPS (375 ML)

A tasty complement for our Chester Salmon Salad (see page 72), but also try it splashed on grilled fish or vegetables.

1½ cups	375 mL	olive oil
2 T	30 mL	shallots, minced
1 tsp	5 mL	garlic, minced
1 tsp	5 mL	fresh thyme, finely chopped
3 T	45 mL	fresh squeezed lemon juice
1 tsp	5 mL	kosher salt
1 T	15 mL	fresh oregano, chopped

In a small saucepan, heat 1/4 cup (60 mL) of the olive oil over medium heat. Add the shallots, garlic and thyme and cook until the shallots are soft, about 3 minutes. Remove the saucepan from the heat and whisk in the lemon juice, salt and remaining olive oil. Let the vinaigrette cool and then stir in the oregano.

Can be stored in a jar in the refrigerator for up to 1 week.

Chive Oil

MAKES 1 CUP (250 ML)

Try drizzling this vibrant oil over scrambled eggs or steamed new potatoes.

1 cup	250 mL	fresh chives, chopped
½ tsp	2 mL	garlic, minced
pinch	pinch	kosher salt
1 cup	250 mL	vegetable oil

In a blender, purée the chives, garlic and salt with the vegetable oil until vibrant green. (To pour out a fine drizzle, put this oil in a squeeze bottle.)

Will keep in the refrigerator for a couple of days.

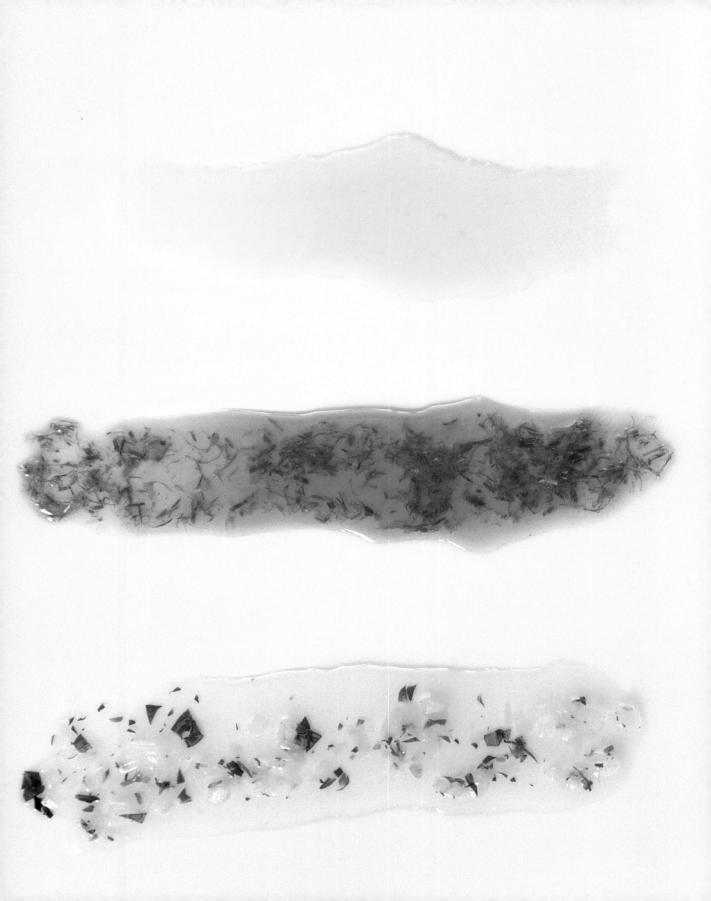

Mess Up Your Plate

Red Onion Marmalade

MAKES 3 CUPS (750 ML)

This is one of our very favourite condiments. For fluffy omelettes, savoury tarts or juicy steaks, we recommend – no, we insist – that you keep some of this in your refrigerator at all times.

⅓ cup	75 mL	olive oil
3 lbs	1.5 kg	red onions (about 6 large), peeled and sliced ⅛" (3 mm) thick
1 T	15 mL	kosher salt
¾ cup	175 mL	white sugar
¾ cup	175 mL	ruby port
¾ cup	175 mL	red wine vinegar
1 T	15 mL	fresh thyme, chopped

In a large pot, heat the olive oil over medium-high heat. Add the red onions and cook until soft, about 7 minutes, stirring frequently. Mix in the salt and sugar and cook for 8 more minutes.

Add the port and red wine vinegar. Bring to a boil, then reduce the heat to low and simmer for 20 minutes until most of the liquid has evaporated. Stir in the thyme.

Can be stored in a tightly sealed container in the refrigerator for several weeks. Best served warm.

Blueberry Green Peppercorn Chutney

MAKES 1 CUP (250 ML)

Although it was created for our Chicken and Waffles (see page 70), we also love to serve this unusual chutney with roasted duck or venison.

1 cup	250 mL	brown sugar, packed
2 T	30 mL	raspberry vinegar
2 T	30 mL	red wine vinegar
2 T	30 mL	white wine vinegar
2 cups	500 mL	blueberries, fresh or frozen
2 T	30 mL	green peppercorns, drained
½ cup	125 mL	onion, finely chopped
1 tsp	5 mL	fresh ginger, finely grated
1½ tsp	7 mL	grated lemon zest
1 T	15 mL	fresh squeezed lemon juice

In a large stainless-steel pot, combine the brown sugar and the vinegars. Cook over medium heat, stirring until the sugar has dissolved. Add the blueberries, green peppercorns, onion, ginger, lemon zest and lemon juice.

Reduce the heat to low, stirring occasionally, and simmer until most of the liquid has evaporated, about 1 hour. The chutney will thicken as it cools.

Can be stored in a tightly sealed container in the refrigerator for several weeks.

Spicy Chipotle Ketchup

MAKES 2 CUPS (500 ML)

This smoky, tangy ketchup gives more of a kick than you'll ever get from a regular bottle of ketchup. Keep it on standby to enjoy with our Rosemary Roasted Potatoes (see page 64) or your favourite sausages.

7 cups	1.75 L	Roma tomatoes (about 12 to 14), chopped
1⅔ cups	400 mL	red pepper (about 2), chopped
1⅓ cups	325 mL	red onion (1 large), chopped
2 cloves	2 cloves	garlic, smashed
½ cup	125 mL	water
½ cup	125 mL	red wine vinegar
2 T	30 mL	chipotle peppers
¼ cup	60 mL	brown sugar, packed
½ tsp	2 mL	kosher salt
½ tsp	2 mL	ground coriander
½ tsp	2 mL	dry mustard
¼ tsp	1 mL	ground ginger

In a large stainless-steel pot, combine the tomatoes, peppers, onions, garlic, water and 1/4 cup (60 mL) of the red wine vinegar. Bring to a boil, then reduce the heat to medium and simmer for 30 minutes, stirring frequently. Remove the pot from the heat and stir in the chipotle peppers. Let the tomato mixture cool completely. In a blender or food processor, purée the tomato mixture in small batches until smooth. Press the purée through a sieve to catch the skins and seeds. Return the purée to the stainless-steel pot. Add the brown sugar, salt, coriander, mustard, ginger and the remaining red wine vinegar. Bring to a boil, then reduce to a simmer, stirring frequently until very thick, about 40 minutes.

Can be stored in a tightly covered container in the refrigerator for up to 2 months.

Pepper Rouille

MAKES 1½ CUPS (375 ML)

Try this fiery mayo on crispy baguette and roast beef sandwiches or dip with frites.

3 large	3 large	egg yolks
2 tsp	10 mL	fresh squeezed lime juice
1 T	30 mL	fresh cilantro leaves
1 tsp	5 mL	garlic, minced
1 tsp	5 mL	sambal
1 tsp	5 mL	kosher salt
1 cup	250 mL	vegetable oil
1	1	roasted red pepper, peeled and seeded

In a food processor, purée the egg yolks, lime juice, cilantro, garlic, sambal and salt until smooth. With the processor running, pour in the oil in a slow, steady stream. The rouille will start to thicken, but be careful not to add the oil too quickly or the mixture could separate. When all the oil has been incorporated, add the roasted pepper and purée until smooth.

Can be stored in a covered container in the refrigerator for up to 3 days.

Tomato Salsa

MAKES 3 CUPS (750 ML)

Nothing beats the flavour of fresh tomato salsa. This recipe is easy to put together and is the perfect complement for eggs, tortillas, steaks and potatoes.

2½ cups	625 mL	Roma tomatoes (about 5), seeded and chopped
½ cup	125 mL	red onion, finely chopped
1	1	jalapeño pepper, minced
2 tsp	10 mL	fresh squeezed lime juice
¼ cup	60 mL	fresh cilantro, chopped
2 T	30 mL	extra virgin olive oil
½ tsp	2 mL	kosher salt

In a small bowl, combine the tomatoes, onion and jalapeño. Stir in the lime juice, cilantro, olive oil and salt.

Can be stored in the refrigerator for up to 2 days. Serve at room temperature for maximum flavour.

Black Olive Pesto

MAKES 1 CUP (250 ML)

Spread this zippy pesto on sandwiches or toss with fresh pasta and extra virgin olive oil.

1 tsp	5 mL	garlic, minced
1 cup	250 mL	Kalamata olives, pitted
½ cup	125 mL	Parmigiano-Reggiano cheese, freshly grated
2 T	30 mL	olive oil

In a food processor, purée the garlic, olives, Parmigiano and olive oil until smooth.

Can be stored in the refrigerator in a tightly covered container for up to a week.

Avocado Crema

MAKES 1 CUP (250 ML)

We like to use Haas avocados for this recipe. Make sure the avocado is nice and ripe for a smooth and tasty crema.

1	1	ripe avocado
1 T	15 mL	fresh squeezed lemon juice
¼ cup	60 mL	sour cream
½ tsp	2 mL	kosher salt

Cut the avocado in half and remove the pit and skin. In a food processor, purée the avocado, lemon juice, sour cream and salt until smooth and creamy.

To store, lay a piece of plastic wrap directly on the crema (this prevents discolouration) and keep in the refrigerator for up to 2 days.

Saffron Aïoli

MAKES 1 CUP (250 ML)

This vibrant sauce is great with grilled fish or vegetables.

1 large	1 large	egg
½ tsp	2 mL	Dijon mustard
1 T	15 mL	fresh squeezed lemon juice
½ tsp	2 mL	garlic, minced
pinch	pinch	saffron
½ tsp	2 mL	kosher salt
1 cup	250 mL	vegetable oil

In a food processor, combine the egg, mustard, lemon juice, garlic, saffron and salt and purée until smooth, about 30 seconds. While the processor is running, pour in the oil in a slow, steady stream. The aïoli will start to thicken slightly. (Be careful not to add the oil too quickly or the mixture could separate.) Keep the aïoli refrigerated until ready to use. The brilliant saffron colour will develop in about an hour. Stir to mix the colour evenly.

Can be stored in a tightly covered container in the refrigerator for up to 3 days.

LET'S GET SAUCY

Dijon Cream Sauce

MAKES 1 CUP (250 ML)

Is the process of making a béarnaise sauce too daunting? Try this sauce over poached eggs and toast instead.

2 cups	500 mL	35% cream
1 T	15 mL	fresh thyme, finely chopped
1 T	15 mL	Dijon mustard
1 T	15 mL	grainy Dijon mustard
pinch	pinch	kosher salt

In a stainless-steel saucepan, combine the cream and thyme. Cook over medium-high heat until reduced by a third. Remove from the heat and whisk in both mustards and salt.

Can be stored in a covered container in the refrigerator for several days.

Always serve this sauce warm. Reheat over a gentle heat, stirring until smooth.

Picante Sauce

MAKES 3 CUPS (750 ML)

We created this zingy tomato sauce to accompany our Chorizo Tortilla (see page 54), but save some for the Roasted Pepper and Basil Strata (see page 62).

¼ cup	60 mL	white wine vinegar
2 T	30 mL	brown sugar, packed
2 tsp	10 mL	kosher salt
1 T	15 mL	fresh ginger, finely grated
1 T	15 mL	garlic, minced
1 tsp	5 mL	yellow mustard seeds
1 tsp	5 mL	cracked black pepper
1 tsp	5 mL	ground cumin
pinch	pinch	saffron
½ tsp	2 mL	cayenne pepper
½ tsp	2 mL	curry paste
¼ cup	60 mL	olive oil
4 cups	1 L	Roma tomatoes (about 8), chopped
1½ cups	375 mL	tomato juice

In a stainless-steel saucepan, combine the vinegar, brown sugar and salt. Bring to a boil, stirring to dissolve the sugar and then remove the pan from the heat. In a small bowl, mix together the ginger, garlic, mustard seeds, pepper, cumin, saffron, cayenne and curry paste. Heat the olive oil in a large pot until it begins to smoke. Carefully stir the spice mix into the hot oil and cook for 2 minutes. Reduce the heat to medium-low and stir in the vinegar mixture, tomatoes and tomato juice, simmering gently for 20 minutes. Cool the Picante Sauce slightly and then purée in batches in a food processor or blender until smooth.

Can be stored in the refrigerator in a tightly covered container for up to 1 week.

Cheesy Parmesan Sauce

MAKES 4 CUPS (1 L)

This sauce is a great staple to have on hand. It freezes beautifully and is a key ingredient in traditional lasagna or cannelloni.

4 cups	1 L	2% milk
⅓ cup	75 mL	unsalted butter
1 clove	1 clove	garlic, crushed
⅓ cup	75 mL	all-purpose flour
⅓ cup	75 mL	Parmigiano-Reggiano cheese, freshly grated
pinch	pinch	ground nutmeg
½ tsp	2 mL	kosher salt

In a saucepan, bring the milk to a boil over medium heat. Remove from the heat and set aside. In a stainless-steel saucepan, melt the butter over low heat. Add the crushed garlic and cook for 2 minutes until fragrant but not brown. Remove the garlic and discard. Whisk in the flour and cook for 4 minutes, stirring constantly to prevent scorching. (This is called a roux, and will have a fragrance like shortbread when it's done.) Slowly pour 1 cup (250 mL) of the hot milk into the roux, whisking constantly. The sauce will begin to thicken. Add the rest of the milk in 1/2 cup (125 mL) increments, continually whisking to prevent lumps. Cook the sauce over low heat for about 8 minutes. With a high-heat spatula, continue stirring to prevent scorching. Remove the pan from the heat. Stir in the Parmigiano-Reggiano, nutmeg and salt. The sauce will thicken considerably as it cools.

Can be stored in the refrigerator for up to a week or frozen for a couple of months. If the sauce has separated in the thawing process, bring it back together by whisking until smooth.

MP Sauce

MAKES 1½ CUPS (375 ML)

Our soon-to-be-famous MP Sauce is a brilliant accompaniment to The Manhandler (see page 64), not to mention hamburgers, eggs or hash browns. Make it on a nice day when you can open up the kitchen window – cooking vinegar can be very unpleasant (really, it'll burn your eyeballs).

1 cup	250 mL	balsamic vinegar
1 cup	250 mL	apple cider vinegar
¼ cup	60 mL	blackstrap molasses
¼ cup	60 mL	corn syrup
1 T	15 mL	soy sauce
⅓ cup	75 mL	shallots, minced
2 T	30 mL	fresh tarragon, finely chopped
1½ tsp	7 mL	garlic, minced
1½ tsp	7 mL	tamarind paste
½ tsp	2 mL	cracked black pepper
½ tsp	2 mL	sambal
1 T	15 mL	chipotle peppers
¼ cup	60 mL	dried dates, pitted and chopped
¼ cup	60 mL	tomato paste
1 tsp	5 mL	Dijon mustard
¼ cup	60 mL	brown sugar, packed
1 tsp	5 mL	kosher salt
¼ tsp	1 mL	baking soda

In a large stainless-steel pot, combine all the ingredients except for the salt and baking soda. Bring the mixture to a boil, then reduce the heat to medium-low and simmer for about 20 minutes, stirring occasionally. Let the mixture cool for at least 15 minutes. In a food processor, purée the sauce. For a smooth finish, press the sauce through a fine sieve. Stir in the salt and baking soda (this will help to balance the acidity of the sauce).

Can be stored in a tightly sealed container in the refrigerator for up to 2 months.

Undercover Eating

CPR Strawberries

MAKES 3 CUPS (750 ML)

Why CPR? Long story. Visit our Web site at www.mildredsays.com.

1½ cups	375 mL	pitted prunes
2½ cups	625 mL	water
1 cup	250 mL	maple syrup
1	1	cinnamon stick
2	2	Granny Smith apples, peeled, cored and cut into ⅛" (3 mm) slices

In a stainless-steel saucepan, combine the prunes, water, maple syrup and cinnamon stick. Simmer over medium heat until the prunes are soft and the liquid is syrupy. Remove the saucepan from the heat, discard the cinnamon stick and mix in the apples.

Can be stored in tightly sealed containers in the refrigerator for up to 2 weeks. Best served warm.

Dark Chocolate Sauce

MAKES 2 CUPS (500 ML)

Chocolate sauce is so simple to make – and so easy to eat. Try it with white, milk or extra-bitter dark chocolate.

1 cup	250 mL	35% cream
12 oz	400 g	best-quality chocolate, finely chopped

In a saucepan, heat the cream until it just begins to boil. Remove the saucepan from the heat and add the chopped chocolate, stirring until smooth and glossy.

Can be stored in a sealed container in the refrigerator for up to 2 weeks. To serve, warm the sauce gently over low heat or microwave for 30 seconds on medium power.

Apple Jack Caramel

MAKES 1 CUP (250 ML)

We love it so much that we drizzle this caramel on our Ice Cream Profiteroles, Ida's Famous French Toast and New York Pecan Squares (see pages 84, 56, 94) – or we eat it straight from the jar (when no one's looking, of course).

1 cup	250 mL	white sugar
2 T	30 mL	water
2 cups	500 mL	apple juice
1	1	cinnamon stick
2	2	whole star anise

Stir the sugar and water together in a saucepan. Place over high heat and boil until the syrup becomes amber in colour. Remove from the heat. At arm's length, slowly whisk in the apple juice, being careful to avoid splatters. Add the cinnamon stick and star anise, return to medium heat and simmer for 20 minutes to allow the flavours to infuse and the sauce to reduce to about 1 cup (250 mL). Let cool and remove the cinnamon stick and star anise.

Can be stored in the refrigerator for several weeks. Best served at room temperature.

Feeling Flaky

Five Star Pastry

MAKES 2 LBS (900 G)

Keep this no-fail pastry recipe on standby, ready to roll, for sweets and savouries. It makes perfect, flaky pastry with a good, buttery flavour.

3 cups	750 mL	all-purpose flour
¼ tsp	1 mL	salt
¼ lb	115 g	unsalted butter, cold
½ lb	227 g	shortening, cold, cut in small cubes
½ cup	125 mL	ice water

Sift the flour and salt into a large mixing bowl.

Using a coarse cheese grater, grate in the cold butter and toss to coat with flour. Drop in the cubed shortening and, with your fingertips, rub it lightly into the flour mixture until all the butter and shortening is broken into small, crumbly pieces resembling coarse breadcrumbs.

Pour the ice water around the edges of the mixture and press together to form a ball. The pastry will be marbled with little flecks of butter and shortening, which will ensure a light and flaky pastry.

Divide the pastry in two, flatten into disks and wrap tightly in plastic wrap. Refrigerate for at least 30 minutes before rolling.

Mildred Says

Here are two suggestions to improve your pastry-making skills.

For starters, cold butter and minimal handling of the dough will make the best pastry, lightest biscuits and flakiest scones. Here's a million dollar tip: Grate the cold butter into the dry ingredients using the coarse side of a cheese grater. This yields small, uniform shavings of butter that incorporate easily, requiring less handling of the dough.

And did you know that your pastry will be flakier if the dough has been frozen first? You can freeze it either lined in a tart shell or as a disk. Either way, wrap the dough tightly with plastic wrap before freezing. When you're ready to use it, defrost the dough completely in the refrigerator. It can be kept in the freezer for up to 3 months.

GLOSSARY

A

AÏOLI A traditional garlic mayonnaise originating in the South of France.

ALMOND EXTRACT A pure essence made with bitter almond oil and alcohol, used for flavouring in pastries and baked goods.

ASIAN PEAR A large, round pear with a pale yellow skin. Often compared to an apple, it has a crisp, firm texture and a sweet, mild flavour. Asian pears should be stored in the refrigerator.

B

BLACKSTRAP MOLASSES A thick, dark syrup with a robust and somewhat bitter-tart flavour. A product of the sugar refining process, it's often used as a sweetener or colouring agent in baked goods such as gingerbread.

BLANCH A cooking technique whereby vegetables and fruits are dunked briefly into boiling water and then plunged immediately into iced water to stop the cooking process. Blanching can be used to loosen the skins of peaches and tomatoes. It can also be used for green vegetables and herbs to quick-cook while preserving their brilliant green colour.

BLIND BAKING Some recipes require pastry shells to be baked before they're filled. Once the pastry has been fitted into the tart shell, it's lined with parchment paper or aluminum foil that extends generously over the sides of the shell to allow for easy removal. Pie weights (or dried beans) are distributed evenly over the parchment or foil. The pastry is then baked until crisp. This minimizes the shrinking of the dough and keeps it from buckling during the baking process.

BLUE POTATOES Long and oval in shape with remarkable purple skin and flesh, these potatoes are available year round. They're also known as Peruvian blue potatoes.

BRIOCHE MOULDS The classic shape for brioche, called brioche à tête, has a fluted base and a pretty top knot. If you want to create this traditional loaf, you can buy special brioche moulds at kitchen supply stores. They also come in individual sizes.

C

CAMPARI A bright red Italian aperitif with a bittersweet flavour, Campari is often mixed with soda for a refreshing summer cocktail.

CAPERS The small buds of a Mediterranean flower that are pickled or brined and usually sold in small jars. They have a salty, acidic taste and are used as a condiment or as a flavouring for savoury sauces.

CELERY ROOT A root vegetable (also known as celeriac) with brown, knotted skin. The taste is a little like parsley, and certainly like celery. Select firm, hard roots about the size of a grapefruit. Celery root should be peeled, and can be eaten raw or cooked.

CELERY SEED This is the seed of a wild celery called lovage, used for flavouring soups, salads and savoury dishes. When we make Caesars, we prefer using celery seed to celery salt (a mixture of celery seed and table salt that often lacks flavour and has the texture of sand). Celery seed has a more robust flavour.

CHIFFONADE A classic French cut that's great for delicate leafy herbs and greens like basil and spinach. It keeps herbs aromatic and leaves brilliant green. To chiffonade, stack the leaves 5 or 6 high and, with a very sharp knife, slice into fine ribbons.

CHIPOTLE PEPPERS Chipotle peppers are smoked jalapeños. They're usually sold in tins with adobo, a spicy tomato-vinegar sauce.

CLAMATO A tomato-based beverage that combines the flavour of onions, celery and spices with clam juice.

COCONUT MILK There's a common misconception that coconut milk is the clear liquid found in fresh coconuts. Actually, it comes from cooking the finely grated white flesh of the coconut with water. A good-quality coconut milk should be thick and creamy. It's available tinned or frozen.

CORNMEAL Dried corn kernels that have been ground into one of three textures – fine, medium or coarse. Cornmeal can be yellow, blue or white, depending on what type of corn is used. It's used for baking and to make polenta.

CRAB MEAT To make crab cakes you can use fresh raw, cooked tinned or frozen crab, as long as the meat is succulent and sweet. If the meat is very wet, squeeze out the excess moisture before making the crab cakes.

CREAM A technique whereby ingredients such as butter and sugar are beaten together until smooth, light and creamy. It's best to use soft butter for this process. Creaming can be done by hand, with a wooden spoon or in an electric mixer fitted with a paddle attachment.

CRIMP The technique used to seal two layers of pastry together. A good seal on your pastry will prevent fillings from spilling out and is a decorative addition to pies and tarts. Crimping can be done with the tines of a fork, the back of a spoon or by pinching the dough together with your fingers. Develop your own signature crimp so that your pies and tarts will always stand out.

CURRY PASTE A mixture of ghee, curry powder, vinegar and other seasonings. It's available in jars and is sold in most food shops.

F

FENNEL A large, pale-green, bulbous vegetable with feathery green fronds. Choose firm, crisp bulbs with fresh tops. Fennel can be eaten raw or cooked. It has a mild, delicate licorice flavour.

FOLD A technique used to gently combine two different mixtures. Folding is best done with a spatula to gently incorporate a lighter mixture into a heavier one (usually beaten egg whites or whipped cream into a batter) while preserving its delicate, airy quality.

G

GREEN PEPPERCORNS Green pepper-corns are tender, unripe black pepper-corns. They have a mild, peppery flavour used to enhance sauces, stews and meats. Green peppercorns are usually packed in brine and sold in small tins or jars.

H

HIGH-HEAT SPATULA These have a moulded plastic handle and head and can withstand high heat. Great for omelette making or any time the spatula may come in contact with a hot surface.

J

JICAMA A large, crunchy root vegetable with a sweet, nutty taste often used in Mexican and South American cookery. It has a thin, brown, papery skin that should be removed before using. Jicama can be eaten raw or cooked.

K

KAFFIR LIME LEAVES The leaves of the kaffir lime tree are glossy, dark green and waxy with an intense citrusy floral fragrance. These are a common ingredient in Thai kitchens and are available in specialty Asian food shops.

KALAMATA OLIVE A very popular Greek, marinated black olive with an almond shape, firm texture and fruity flavour.

KOSHER SALT An additive-free, flaky-grained salt. We prefer to use kosher salt for seasoning, since it has a mild flavour and is easily sprinkled. We use regular table salt for baking, however. Kosher salt is generally less salty than table or sea salts.

L

LIMONATA A sparkling, slightly tart lemonade. We prefer the San Pellegrino brand, which is available in Italian specialty food shops.

M

MATCHSTICK A small, even, stick-shaped cut of fruit or vegetable, usually about 2" (5 cm) long by 1/8" (3 mm) thick.

N

NIÇOISE OLIVE This small, round Provençal olive ranges in colour from purple to black. It has a mellow, nutty flavour and is an essential ingredient in Niçoise salad.

O

OAT BRAN The outer layer of the oat. It's available in a fine, flaked form and is used for baking. Oat bran is a high-fibre addition to cereals and granolas.

OMELETTE PAN Pans for omelettes should have a flat, heavy bottom for even cooking and slightly sloped sides to allow the eggs to roll out. Stainless-steel and cast-iron omelette pans need to be seasoned for optimum use, but some pans come with non-stick finishes.

ORANGE OIL A highly concentrated, pure extract made from the oils in the zest of the orange. It comes in small bottles that should be refrigerated once opened. Orange oil is available in specialty grocery shops.

P

PANKO Flaky, white, unseasoned breadcrumbs used in Japanese cooking to coat foods that are fried. They create a light, crispy texture and can be used anywhere you'd normally use breadcrumbs.

PARCHMENT PAPER An uncoated baking paper used to line baking sheets and pans to prevent sticking. It's sold in precut sheets and rolls.

PECTIN A natural substance found in the seeds, skin and core of many types of fruit. It's used to thicken jams and preserves. Pectin is available in liquid and powdered form, but the two aren't necessarily interchangeable.

PIE WEIGHTS Small metal or ceramic beads used for weighting down dough when blind baking. A true luxury item, since dried beans will do the same job.

PIPING BAG A plastic or canvas conical-shaped bag used to dispense batters, icings and whipped cream. These bags come in many sizes and can be fitted with a variety of piping tips that give different results when decorating.

PIPING TIP A small, cone-shaped tip made of metal or plastic that fits the piping bag. The tips come in a variety of shapes for decorative designs. The number indicates the size of the opening at the end of the tip.

POLENTA An Italian dish made by cooking cornmeal with a liquid (usually water, stock or cream). It can be served smooth and creamy or firm and fried.

PREPARED JARS Jars used for storing preserves and condiments must be clean, dry and sterilized to avoid contamination. Jars can be sterilized by boiling or heating them in the oven. They can be stored in the refrigerator or, when closed with a proper seal, kept at room temperature for many months.

PUNCH DOWN A technique used to deflate yeasted dough so that it can rise again. These multiple risings help mellow the yeasty flavour by causing the dough to rise more than once. Use your fist to punch down and deflate the dough.

R

RAMEKIN A small porcelain or earthenware baking dish, usually 3" (7.5 cm) to 4" (10 cm) in diameter. Ramekins are used for crème brûlées and baked eggs.

RASP A traditional woodworking tool that's been modified for use in the kitchen as a very fine grater. It has very sharp teeth and is perfect for mincing garlic, zesting citrus fruits and grating hard cheeses.

RICE VINEGAR A type of vinegar made from fermented rice. Japanese rice vinegar, which we prefer, has a pale yellow colour and a sweet, mild flavour.

ROASTED GARLIC Roasting garlic gives it a mellow, slightly sweet flavour. We suggest wrapping peeled garlic cloves in a piece of aluminum foil (which keeps it extra moist and easy to portion) and roasting at 375°F (190°C) for 20 to 30 minutes (or until the garlic is very soft). Add roasted garlic to tarts, omelettes and mashed potatoes.

ROASTED PEPPER Roasting peppers brings out their flavour and sweetness. To roast a pepper perfectly, place the whole pepper on a baking sheet in a 375°F (190°C) oven for 35 to 40 minutes until it's slightly charred and blistered. Carefully transfer the pepper to a small bowl and cover tightly with plastic wrap. The trapped steam will loosen the skin, making peeling easier. When the pepper is cool enough to handle, peel off the skin with your fingers and discard the seeds and stem.

ROLLED OATS Rolled oats are oat groats that have been steamed, rolled and flattened so that they cook quickly. Rolled oats come in a variety of flakes – quick-cook, old-fashioned and instant. For our recipes we like to use old-fashioned rolled oats because we prefer their flavour and texture.

S

SAFFRON The brilliant orange stigma hand-picked from the purple crocus flower. This costly spice is used to add flavour and colour to dishes. Fine saffron is sold in threads in tiny envelopes (a little saffron goes a long way).

SAMBAL A hot, spicy condiment usually made of red chilies, vinegar and salt. It comes in jars and is sold in most Asian food shops.

SAUTÉ To cook food quickly over high heat in a skillet or shallow frying pan using a minimal amount of oil.

SEASON To season a skillet or omelette pan, lightly coat the inside surface with vegetable oil and place over low heat for about 20 minutes. The oil adheres to the pan, smoothing out the surface and creating a stick-resistant finish. Frequent use and minimal washing will maintain the pan's seasoned finish.

SEGMENT To segment citrus fruits, slice the top and bottom off the fruit. Using a serrated paring knife, slice the peel from the fruit until you're right down to the flesh. To separate the segments from the membrane, slice down to the core on either side of each segment. These skinless, seedless segments are perfect for salads when a juicy bite of fruit is desired.

SERRATED KNIFE This knife has a scalloped edge that's ideal for slicing breads, cakes and soft fruits and vegetables.

SIFT To pass dry ingredients through a fine-mesh sieve (or sifter) in order to remove any lumps and to aerate ingredients.

SPIDER This large, open-mesh scoop with a long handle is ideal for removing foods from deep-fryers or pots of boiling water.

SPRINGFORM PAN A round baking pan with a removable bottom and a clasp that opens up the sides for easy removal of the baked item.

SQUEEZE BOTTLE Soft plastic bottles with removable screw tops that have a conical tip that can be cut to various openings. Ideal for drizzling sauces, oils and caramel.

STAR ANISE A star-shaped spice that's dark brown in colour, star anise is commonly used for its aromatic licorice flavour. It's available whole or ground.

T

TAMARIND Sometimes known as Indian date, tamarind is the sour lemony pulp of a fruit grown widely in India, Africa and Asia. The dried, leathery pulp is reconstituted in water and the seeds and skins are strained out. Tamarind pulp comes in jars or

small bricks and is available in Indian and Asian food shops.

TOASTING NUTS Toasting brings out natural flavour and crunch. Spread the nuts in a single layer on a baking sheet and toast in a 350°F (180°C) oven for 7 to 10 minutes, giving them a shake halfway through.

V

VANILLA BEAN The dried fruit pod of an edible orchid. The long, thin pod filled with tiny black seeds contains an aromatic vanilla flavour. Splitting the pod exposes the seeds for maximum flavour. The seeds may be eaten, but the pod is usually discarded.

VANILLA EXTRACT A vanilla-infused essence commonly used to flavour baked goods. Pure vanilla extract is preferable to artificially flavoured vanilla extract.

Y

YEAST Yeast is a living substance that needs moisture and warmth to activate. We use fresh yeast in our recipes because we like the flavour it imparts, but you can easily substitute dry yeast at a 1 to 2 ratio. For example, 2 T (30 mL) of fresh yeast equals 1 T (15 mL) of dry yeast. Fresh yeast comes in compressed cakes and should be moist, sweet smelling and even coloured. It's highly perishable and should be stored in the refrigerator. To wake up your yeast, dissolve it in warm water, about 100°F (50°C). Set the mixture aside in a warm place for 5 to 10 minutes, at which point it should be active, foamy and ready to use.

Z

ZEST The brightly coloured skin of citrus fruits containing pure, concentrated oils. When zesting lemons, oranges or limes, use a rasp or zester to remove only the brightly coloured outer peel, and not the white pith, which is very bitter.

INDEX

THANKS

When we first considered the notion of a Mildred Pierce cookbook, we began sifting through the boxes of old menus and scraps of paper and notebooks that archived our precious, stained and tattered recipes. What we discovered was a history of the evolution of Mildred Pierce Restaurant – the tireless vision of our dear friends, Ted and Ivan, who never doubted Mildred Pierce for a moment, Kevin Gallagher's constant presence in the dining room, Anne Yarymowich's vocal concerts coming off the front line to a packed house, so many waiters who gave up their acting careers to better serve our customers, photos of many happy hours spent with the staff at beloved Bungalow Island and all the customers who have continued to come to us over the years. But there are many wonderful people whose support and encouragement have helped this delightful book come together.

KEVIN GALLAGHER, proprietor of Mildred Pierce Restaurant, consummate brunch host and cribbage partner; MARTHA ARIMA, tireless recipe tester and stickler for details; ANNE YARYMOWICH, first chef of Mildred Pierce Restaurant and brunch pioneer, distiller of rose petal-infused vodka for inspiration and lots of laughs about the good old days; LIANNE GEORGE for helping Mildred find her voice; SUSAN MCINTEE AND NICK MONTELEONE and the staff of 52 Pick-up Inc. for their vision and spectacular design work; SARA BORINS, SHANNON CONWAY AND KAREN PRESS at Otherwise Editions for keeping the project on the rails, particularly through the hairy corners; DOUGLAS BRADSHAW AND EDWARD POND, photographers extraordinaire and long-standing patrons of Mildred Pierce Restaurant; HOLLY FARRELL for her stunning paintings and patience; THE KITCHEN AND DINING ROOM STAFF (past and present) at Mildred Pierce Restaurant, who continue to make us shine; SEGAR, RAVI AND VERA, who have cracked eggs, mixed pancake batter and squeezed orange juice from the beginning (and always with a smile); THE STAFF at The Cookworks for picking up the slack when Claire and Donna affixed themselves to the computer for days on end; KAREN ALLISTON for copy editing, over and over and over; RICK ARCHBOLD for putting it all in perspective; JAY MANDARINO for ink and paper; MAR AND FRANK for never losing faith in the seemingly endless ventures that their children take them on; RORY AND MAEVE, born and bred in the restaurant biz and orphaned on most Sundays, until they were old enough to work that is; PETER AND ANN for punctuation, grammar and copper pipes cut into baking tins; HELEN for looking after Lucy and Sophie; and DOMINIC for renovating Claire's house while she worked on this book.

AND ALL THE LOYAL CUSTOMERS WHO HAVE FREQUENTED MILDRED PIERCE RESTAURANT OVER THE PAST FOURTEEN YEARS.